OYSTER

Edible

Series Editor: Andrew F. Smith

EDIBLE is a revolutionary series of books dedicated to food and drink that explores the rich history of cuisine. Each book reveals the global history and culture of one type of food or beverage.

Already published

Apple Erika Janik, *Avocado* Jeff Miller, *Banana* Lorna Piatti-Farnell, *Barbecue* Jonathan Deutsch and Megan J. Elias, *Beans* Nathalie Rachel Morris, *Beef* Lorna Piatti-Farnell, *Beer* Gavin D. Smith, *Berries* Heather Arndt Anderson, *Biscuits and Cookies* Anastasia Edwards, *Brandy* Becky Sue Epstein, *Bread* William Rubel, *Breakfast Cereal* Kathryn Cornell Dolan, *Cabbage* Meg Muckenhoupt, *Cake* Nicola Humble, *Caviar* Nichola Fletcher, *Champagne* Becky Sue Epstein, *Cheese* Andrew Dalby, *Chillies* Heather Arndt Anderson, *Chocolate* Sarah Moss and Alexander Badenoch, *Cocktails* Joseph M. Carlin, *Coconut* Constance L. Kirker and Mary Newman, *Cod* Elisabeth Townsend, *Coffee* Jonathan Morris, *Corn* Michael Owen Jones, *Curry* Colleen Taylor Sen, *Dates* Nawal Nasrallah, *Doughnut* Heather Delancey Hunwick, *Dumplings* Barbara Gallani, *Edible Flowers* Constance L. Kirker and Mary Newman, *Edible Insects* Gina Louise Hunter, *Eggs* Diane Toops, *Fats* Michelle Phillipov, *Figs* David C. Sutton, *Foie Gras* Norman Kolpas, *Game* Paula Young Lee, *Gin* Lesley Jacobs Solmonson, *Hamburger* Andrew F. Smith, *Herbs* Gary Allen, *Herring* Kathy Hunt, *Honey* Lucy M. Long, *Hot Dog* Bruce Kraig, *Hummus* Harriet Nussbaum, *Ice Cream* Laura B. Weiss, *Jam, Jelly and Marmalade* Sarah B. Hood, *Lamb* Brian Yarvin, *Lemon* Toby Sonneman, *Liqueur* Lesley Jacobs Solmonson, *Lobster* Elisabeth Townsend, *Melon* Sylvia Lovegren, *Milk* Hannah Velten, *Moonshine* Kevin R. Kosar, *Mushroom* Cynthia D. Bertelsen, *Mustard* Demet Güzey, *Nuts* Ken Albala, *Offal* Nina Edwards, *Olive* Fabrizia Lanza, *Onions and Garlic* Martha Jay, *Oranges* Clarissa Hyman, *Oyster* Carolyn Tillie, *Pancake* Ken Albala, *Pasta and Noodles* Kantha Shelke, *Pickles* Jan Davison, *Pie* Janet Clarkson, *Pineapple* Kaori O'Connor, *Pizza* Carol Helstosky, *Pomegranate* Damien Stone, *Pork* Katharine M. Rogers, *Potato* Andrew F. Smith, *Pudding* Jeri Quinzio, *Rice* Renee Marton, *Rum* Richard Foss, *Saffron* Ramin Ganeshram, *Salad* Judith Weinraub, *Salmon* Nicolaas Mink, *Sandwich* Bee Wilson, *Sauces* Maryann Tebben, *Sausage* Gary Allen, *Seaweed* Kaori O'Connor, *Shrimp* Yvette Florio Lane, *Soda and Fizzy Drinks* Judith Levin, *Soup* Janet Clarkson, *Spices* Fred Czarra, *Sugar* Andrew F. Smith, *Sweets and Candy* Laura Mason, *Tea* Helen Saberi, *Tequila* Ian Williams, *Tomato* Clarissa Hyman, *Truffle* Zachary Nowak, *Vanilla* Rosa Abreu-Runkel, *Vodka* Patricia Herlihy, *Water* Ian Miller, *Whiskey* Kevin R. Kosar, *Wine* Marc Millon, *Yoghurt* June Hersh

Oyster

A Global History

Carolyn Tillie

REAKTION BOOKS

Published by Reaktion Books Ltd
Unit 32, Waterside
44–48 Wharf Road
London N1 7UX, UK
www.reaktionbooks.co.uk

First published 2017
Copyright © Carolyn Tillie 2017

Printed and bound in India by Replika Press Pvt. Ltd

A catalogue record for this book is available from the British Library

ISBN 978 1 78023 817 3

Contents

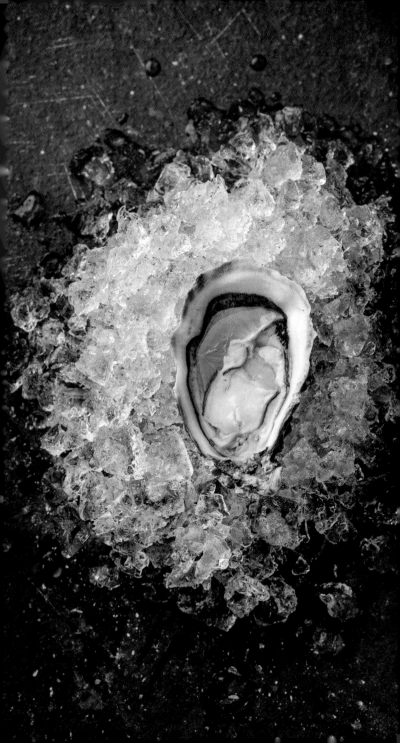

Introduction

In the mid-1970s, as a twelve-year-old, I was taken to New Orleans by my parents to meet my Aunt Lola, one of my father's five sisters. In the early 1960s, my Aunt Lola left her Georgia-born family, moved to the heart of the French Quarter, and worked as a Playboy bunny at one of the earliest of Hugh Hefner's clubs devoted to female pulchritude. I remember flipping through her scrapbook of pictures and memorabilia, gazing at pictures of her with the likes of Bob Hope and Omar Sharif. I didn't understand most of what I was looking at, but inherently comprehended that – like the fictional Auntie Mame – Aunt Lola was a woman who was full of vitality, energy and an aura of *joie de vivre* I found very compelling. During the 1960s the New Orleans Playboy Club – a converted old carriage house – sat on Iberville Street in the same block as Felix's Oyster Bar and the Acme Oyster House. What I didn't know then, but understand now, is how this confluence of food and sex established a vortex in which my Aunt Lola thrived.

On our first night in New Orleans, she took us to Antoine's Restaurant, one of the oldest dining establishments in America, where she 'knew some people'. Winking at me, she ordered an oyster appetizer platter for the table to share

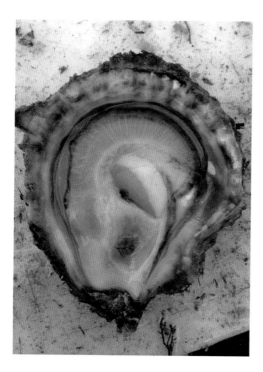

Irish oyster from Galway Bay.

while we perused the menu to decide our entrée choices. On the table arrived a heaping tower of food, including Oysters Rockefeller, Oysters Thermidor, fried oysters and raw oysters on the half shell. With trepidation, I ate a fried oyster (what kid doesn't like fried food?). Not bad, I thought. Intrigued with the raw oysters, I copied Aunt Lola and drizzled a little mignonette atop the glistening greyness held inside the half-open shell, and followed my gorgeous aunt's every move as she taught me how to eat my first raw oyster. Hold it in the mouth, chew a little, taste the delicacy of the sea. In her fifties, Aunt Lola garnered attention from those around her, and my twelve-year-old brain didn't know that what she exuded was pure 'sex appeal', but somehow it translated to

8

the consumption of these oysters that she enjoyed with such gusto. Such was the joy of my new gastronomic discovery that evening that instead of some other entrée, my father let me order more oysters as a main meal. I idolized my aunt and I wanted to be just like her and my transmutation could only occur by the ingestion of the magical bivalve.

Volumes have been written about this humble little creature; romantic favours extolled, great empires built and new lands discovered all because of this ancient shellfish. It is one of the oldest foods consumed by humans. At various

Pacific oyster, waiting for shucking.

points in history, the oyster has been the food of the rich and the sustenance of the poor. Various medicinal qualities were ascribed to it, with some physicians claiming it acted as an aphrodisiac while others said that it cooled the blood and related passions. It has been cooked in various ways, both simple and ornate, used as stuffing and eaten raw in all its glorious simplicity. It is, quite frankly, the perfect food.

I

Definition and Science

The oyster is a magical animal, an ancient creature that has changed very little in the last two hundred million years. It is simple-looking with a complex life cycle. Generally, oysters start off male and settle into femaleness later in life. Most can change their gender and are considered protandrous (first, male) hermaphrodites, with some genera, like *Ostrea edulis*, the common European oyster, alternating back-and-forth throughout their entire lives. While it appears to be a singularly simple grey blob, the oyster actually has a heart, lungs, kidneys and colourless blood. Yet with no brain, it is a marvel of engineering for operating as a filter – it can help clean the body of water in which it lives. The oyster is one of the oldest sources of food known to man and is considered a superfood. Naturally high in essential vitamins and minerals including protein, iron, omega-3 fatty acids, calcium and zinc, the oyster also contains vitamins A, B1 (thiamine), B2 (riboflavin), B3 (niacin), C (ascorbic acid) and D2 (calciferol). They are low in fat and highly nutritious. The encasing shell consists of 75 per cent calcium phosphate (calcite), calcium sulphate (gypsum), magnesium, aluminium salts and iron oxide. Assisting in bone growth, the shells are often ground up as a nutritional supplement for pregnant women who suffer from a calcium deficiency.

The English term 'oyster' first appeared in the fourteenth century as *ostre*, or Anglo-Norman *oistre*, which stems from either the Latin *ostrea* or Greek ὄστρεον (meaning 'bone'), probably based on the hardness of the outer shell. Technically belonging to the Mollusca family – members of which are invertebrates that have one or more segments that completely or partially enclose the body to protect it from predators – the oyster is a bivalve. That is, there are two halves that create the whole, but neither half of its external self is symmetrical. The external shell of every oyster species is rounded on one end and pointed on the other. That pointed end – known as the beak or umbo – conceals the hinge, which has small teeth that allow the valve to align and close properly. Inside the surface is a ligament known as the adductor muscle, which exerts from 10 to 16 kg (22 to 35 lb) of pressure, keeping the two

The tell-tale black spot on the inside of an oyster is where the adductor muscle attaches itself to the shell.

Oysters come in a wide variety of sizes, from long and thin to wide and fat. Depicted here, from left to right, are: (first row) Delaware Bay, Belon, Old 1871, Blue Point; (second row) Quilcene, Hollywood, Willapa and Mirada; (third row) Reach Island, Westport, Penn Cove, Shigoku and Miyagi.

valves together. It is that adductor muscle which leaves the dark spot on the inside of the shell and is used by scientists to identify the oyster's taxonomic classification. Looking at a closed oyster, there is a flatter side – which is considered the right-hand side – while the deeper, cup-shaped portion is the left-hand side.

The adductor muscle is critical for the oyster's survival. It is that muscle that carefully manipulates the two sides of the bivalve to open and close as needed. For the adductor muscle to function properly, it must receive a constant supply of oxygenated blood. Without the ability to open and close at appropriate intervals, the oyster will suffocate, starve and die. When the oyster feeds, it opens its mantle just enough – 2 to 3 mm – to let in some water current while still keeping out predators. A bit of minuscule plankton is strained out of the water by the gills and it is upon these tiny organisms that the oyster feeds. Cilia separate out unwanted matter, then the adductor muscle contracts the mantle and forces out the water, readying for the process again. A live oyster can remain closed for up to a month, which is beneficial for the consumer, as it is possible to keep live oysters in one's own refrigerator for a week or two (assuming it takes this long for them to be harvested and transported via distributors). It just needs to remain moist – in a damp towel, for example.

There are many oysters which are grown for non-edible reasons: specifically, pearl oysters from the Pteriidae family (cultivated for their ability to create a semi-precious gem-stone); types of spiny or thorny oysters like the *Spondylus* from the Spondylidae family (used in the production of ceramics for the replacement of silica); and the windowpane oyster from the Placunidae family, which, although technically edible (like all these oysters), is valued more for its translucent shell and is used in the manufacture of glues and varnishes. True oysters belong to the order and family of Ostreidae and the genera include *Ostrea*, *Crassostrea* and *Saccostrea*. These classifi-cations are based on the size and shape of the oyster in its larval state, how it reproduces, its lifespan, morphology and adult shell shape. When a foreign object – such as a grain of sand – makes its way inside an oyster, it tries to protect the soft, fleshy part of its body by slowly coating the infestation. Thus a pearl is created. Humans can consume pearl oysters, but the meat inside their shells is flimsy and thin with minimal flavour. Also, a pearl can be created in a true oyster, whose body is made of calcite, but these pearls tend to be misshapen and of poor quality as they are lustreless concretions of calcite with little value. The Pteriidae oysters have an internal shell of nacre that is of higher quality than its Ostreidae cousin's, with the added bonus of being iridescent. 'Pearls' have been

A spiny or thorny oyster, the spondylus, while edible, is more known for its decorative uses and was a symbol of power and fertility in pre-Hispanic societies.

discovered in other molluscs, such as conch shells, clams and scallops, but are similarly composed of the worthless calcite.

An important feature of the mollusc family is that its members use the same organ for multiple purposes: the heart and nephridia (the invertebrate version of kidneys) are part of the reproductive system; the gills 'breathe' and create a flowing water current through their mantle which is necessary for excretion and reproduction. Sometimes they can change gender as needed. There are some oysters that fertilize their own eggs, as their gonads contain both sperm and eggs; male and female oysters of the *Crassostrea* genus spawn simultaneously, the male releasing his sperm and the female releasing millions upon millions of eggs. When sperm and egg meet, they join to become a fertilized egg or larva. Being transsexual, a *Crassostrea* will start its existence as a male but will change to become a female during the next season and continue to change its sex several times over the span of its existence. Species of the *Ostrea* genus, such as European and Olympia flat oysters, are bi-sexual, changing sexes several times in a single spawning season. The ova are created and remain within the shell when spawning begins during the oyster's female stage. As a male, it releases its sperm into the water and this subsequently enters the female shell to fertilize the eggs. This fertilized egg stays in the parent's shell and incubates for several days before being released as free-swimming larvae.

The oyster is very particular about where and when it will reproduce. The open sea is too cold and turbulent. Oysters like areas of brackish water, where a bit of fresh water mixes

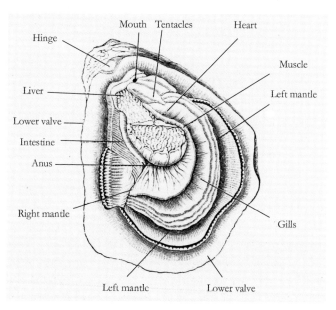

The anatomy of an oyster.

Fossilized oyster from the Jurassic period – 150 million years old – from the Cajamarca Formation, Peru.

with salty seawater: bays, estuaries or reefs. Salinity must be between 2 and 3 per cent and the temperature needs to be at least 10°C (50°F), so these births tend to occur very early in the spring. When a female oyster becomes fertilized, she releases 100 million baby oyster larvae that swim about for approximately two weeks trying to avoid predators, such as other fish in the water looking for a meal. One in ten thousand of these baby larvae survive their childhood journey and attach themselves to a substrate; a string, a twig or another oyster. They are now known as 'spat' and measure about 25 mm (1 in.) in size. Before becoming fully fledged oysters, they discard those parts of their body that helped them get to where they are: the eye that showed the direction to travel, the cilia that helped them move and the foot which they used to grapple on to their new home. They do this by means of byssus filaments, a sort of powerful cement that enables the oyster to permanently attach themselves to rocks or substrate so they can't be picked up or carried away as they grow from their post-larval life to adulthood. Inedible, the byssus is referred to as the 'beard' and is removed before cooking.

This teenage oyster, settling in for the first year until adulthood, is a male. But for this first summer, he spends his time breathing in up to 230 litres (50 gallons) of water a day, straining out the plankton for his meal with his gills, spitting out what doesn't taste good and fertilizing hundreds of thousands of eggs. This explains why eating oysters in the summer has historically not been recommended. An oyster working this hard to create and expel sperm becomes milky and flabby, affecting its taste, as 75 per cent of its body weight is sacrificed to reproduction. Modern aquaculture has made this practice moot, but old habits die hard. Historically those months without an 'R' in their spelling – May, June, July and August – were the times to avoid oyster consumption, as that was peak reproduction period. After the spawning period, the oyster goes back to being just an eating and filtering machine as it starts to plump up again to that desirable consumable we know and love. If the oyster's living environment starts to get colder – around 4 to 7°C (40 to 45°F) – it will lie dormant, because its digestive system ceases to function. The oyster hibernates until the waters begin to warm again. Many oysters that spawn year-round in warm waters (such as those in the Gulf of Mexico) make for less desirable eating as they become fatty, watery, soft and less flavourful. At one year old, the male oyster feels the need to procreate and may become a female, if it wants to.

Today, 95 per cent of the world's oysters are commercially farmed. Farming has been unusually successful at preserving both the species and the environment in which they live. Unlike farmed fish, oysters do not pollute the water; in fact, they clean it by absorbing and filtering minerals and nutrients that otherwise could cause algal blooms. Oysters assist other wildlife by removing nitrogen from the water, improving clarity and assisting in building sustainability in their waters. As an oyster can only grow and thrive in healthy and clean locations, oyster farmers are motivated to protect their environment by refraining from the use of chemicals. While there are still some farmers who go into natural oyster beds to collect wild larvae, in modern oyster aquafarming most replicate the natural early life cycle in hatcheries, where the larvae are cared for and given appropriate microalgal nutrients to thrive. The larvae are suspended on a substrate or 'cultch' in tanks of circulating water until the larvae grow into spat size and can be referred to as 'seed'. They are moved into progressively larger tanks as they grow until they are ready for the 'grow-out' phase where they can be transferred to the ocean. Most oysters require two to three years from spawning to table.

There are three different ways to cultivate the oyster from seed. Small oysters – measuring about 6 to 12 mm in length – may be strewn over existing oyster beds. This is the closest process to historical fishing methods for wild oysters as the oysters are left alone to mature naturally and are dredged up later. In the second method, the substrate – with its attached baby oysters – can be placed within bags, racks or cages. In areas where the seabed is too deep, rafts are used to keep the oysters in their racks or bags suspended with flotation devices; otherwise the containers are planted on the ocean floor for monitoring and sorting. The third method uses an artificial maturation tank for a variety of reasons: there may not be an acceptable natural ocean area for expansive cultivation, there may exist predators or poachers that would be a

A modern oyster bed in New South Wales, Australia.

deterrent to natural farming, and the tank offers better control of temperature and salinity that aids in the growth rate of the oyster. Predators include starfish, which wrap themselves around an oyster and pry it open for its meat, as well as stingrays, stone crabs and birds such as oystercatchers and gulls.

Oysters left to their own devices may grow in clusters and it is not surprising to see smaller oysters attached to larger ones in markets. To prevent this, throughout an oyster's lifespan – before heading to market – they are sorted and 'culled'. Many farms utilize motorized dredges to gather oyster-filled bags or cages, but in some locations where the bay is only a few feet deep and wild oysters still live, the workers resort to a centuries-old technique of scooping the oysters into the shift with long, wooden-handled tongs. Oyster boats are shallow and wide and the tonging is heavy, back-breaking

A culling hammer is used to measure whether an oyster has grown to a marketable size.

Baby oysters are known as 'spat'.

work. When the boat is full, the farmer will begin the culling process. Using a special culling hammer, similar to a small ball-pein hammer, the worker will deftly strike and eliminate attached shells or even baby oysters without damaging the marketable oyster. Antique culling hammers like the one pictured and used on the East Coast of the United States include a shell gauge which measures exactly 7.6 cm (3 in.) to indicate the acceptable size at which an oyster may be harvested. If the oyster is smaller than the acceptable range, back into the water it goes.

Depending on the genus, mature, edible oysters range from 2 to 18 cm (1 to 7 in.). There have been claims of oysters as large as dinner plates before modern cultivation techniques started managing their growth cycles. The Pacific oyster reaches its market size in 9 to 24 months, while the Kumamoto needs at least 24 to 60 months for marketability. Oyster growers on the Pacific coast who have decades-old oyster beds claim to have seen numerous oysters that have been living and thriving for more than twenty years. Edible oysters come in many different varieties of size, shape and flavour and those variables change dramatically with how and where they are grown, the water temperature and cultivation techniques.

Crassostrea gigas is the most widely commercially grown and cultivated oyster in the world and accounts for more than 75 per cent of the world's edible oysters. It is often known as the Pacific oyster, the Japanese oyster or the Miyagi. It is easy to farm, tolerant of environmental changes and amenable to changing locations. Its spat has been transferred all over the world, from its point of origin in Japan, to the Pacific coast of the United States in the early twentieth century and to the shores of France in the mid-1960s. It is this oyster which has been credited with saving a worldwide oyster industry.

SOME OF THE MOST BASIC AND
WELL-KNOWN EDIBLE VARIETIES

Genera	Species	Common names
Crassostrea	*angulata*	Portuguese
	ariakensis	Suminoe, Sumo, Chinese
	gasar	Mangrove, Gasar cupped
	gigas	Pacific, Japanese, Miyagi, Fanny Bay, Kusshi
	virginica	Eastern, Atlantic, Malpeque, PEI, Wellfleet, Blue Point
Ostrea	*edulis*	European flat, Belon, Colchester flat
	sikamea	Kumamoto, Kumi
	chilensis	Chilean
	conchaphila	Olympia, Oly
Saccostrea	*glomerata*	Sydney rock

Many historical oyster beds suffered dwindling inventory due to overfishing or disease until saved by the introduction of the Pacific oyster. This oyster has also been able to create entirely new industries in locales that had not previously farmed oysters.

2
Prehistoric and Ancient History

Before dinosaurs roamed the earth, 234 million years ago, there were oysters. From palaeontologists – those who study fossils – we learn of the oyster's extensive history. Archaeologists, who examine human artefacts and remains, and anthropologists, who investigate cultures and ancient societies, all research ancient oysters. All three of these sciences rely on oyster excavations for their data. Fossilized oyster beds are known as 'middens', a word from the early Scandinavian or Norwegian word *mødding* (domestic waste dump). These excavations help detail the diet, living situations and societal habits of ancient peoples. One difficulty in researching the oyster's history is taxonomy; as late as the 1950s, the now-famous Pacific oyster, *Crassostrea gigas*, was known as *Ostrea laperousii*. The classification of the primordial oyster by scientists is a Herculean task, as a singular oyster living alone atop a lone rock will lead a different life from that of its brother who exists on the soft bottom of the ocean, nestled among its kin. When oysters grow in crowded conditions – competing for resources – their shells change shape. The majority of palaeontologists agree that four broad divisions of the Ostreidae may be recognized: *Ostrea*, *Alectryon*, *Exogyra* and *Gryphaea*. The oldest oyster fossils date to the Triassic period (about 248 to

Giant Upper Cretaceous Ostreidae of the Gulf Coast and Caribbean, *c.* 100 to 66 million years ago.

NEW UPPER CRETACEOUS OSTREIDAE FROM THE GULF REGION.

213 million years ago) and have been excavated in the Kolyma River basin in far eastern Siberia, Ellesmere Island in Arctic Canada, the Rocky Mountain foothills in British Columbia, the Cedar Mountains in west-central Nevada, and in eastern Sicily, Italy. These fossils have been classified as *Gryphaea*. The *Gryphaea* and *Exogyra* genera are known for their tightly curled shape which evolved as a protective strategy against prey. Small predators such as the snail or starfish would bore through the shell to eat the flesh or birds would carry them into the sky and drop them, hoping the shattering of the shell would release the succulent treat. Eventually mammals would evolve with grinding teeth suitable for chomping through the oyster's protective shell.

There is no major landmass on Earth where some form of fossilized oyster has not been found. Great shell middens in Denmark date from the Stone Age and include oysters alongside mussels, cockles, periwinkles and snails. Scattered along the western shores of Europe, oyster middens can be found in Scotland, Brittany and Tunisia. In America, they were discovered along the western Pacific shores in California and along the Atlantic in Maine. In Texas, an archaeological dig more than 1.2 km (4,000 ft) deep to the Cretaceous strata produced a surprisingly large variety of oysters, from the minute *Exogyra arietina* less than 3 cm (1 in.) in length, to the gigantic *Exogyra ponderosa* shells, which can weigh 2 kg (5 lb) or more. In South America, excavations in the Andes mountains of Peru at the Cajamarca Formation – now 2.7 km (9,000 ft) above sea level – have unearthed oysters from the Miocene period (23 to 5 million years ago).

The human appetite for oysters over these centuries may be judged by the fact that at places like Lake Diana in Corsica

Gryphaea, otherwise known as Devil's Toenails, owing to their curved, evil-looking demeanour.

and Saint-Michel-en-l'herme in the Vendée, there exist islands formed entirely of discarded oyster shells. In Britain, the most common oyster fossils date to the Jurassic period and are known as *Gryphaea arcuata*. These oysters flourished from about 227 to 151 million years ago but were first noticed by humans during the medieval era. One of the contributing factors to *Gryphaea*'s extinction may have been its shape: the extreme coiling would have prevented it from opening and reproducing efficiently. Commonly found around Suffolk and Gloucestershire, these fossils became known as Devil's Toenails owing to their curved, demonic-like appearance and the belief that each was a discarded toenail of Satan himself. The motif appears in the coat of arms of the town of Scunthorpe, in North Lincolnshire where the evil-looking fossil remains were known to have been found. Apothecaries in the seventeenth and eighteenth centuries would grind up these fossils and prescribe the consumption of the powder as a curative for joint pain. This may have had some basis in fact: calcium-rich shells are now recommended by some dieticians for osteoporosis.

The oldest evidence of mass oyster consumption dates back 164,000 years to Mossel Bay in South Africa, now known as 'The Point of Human Origins', where oyster farming continues to this day. Aboriginal peoples in Australia – arguably the oldest living culture on earth – have archaeological middens ascribed to them, which were built up over thousands of years, 40,000 to 60,000 years ago. The Ngaro aborigines, who inhabited the Whitsunday Islands and coastal regions of Queensland from at least 7000 BC up to their resettlement in the 1800s, are associated with the cave openings and shell middens that are still visible along the steep slopes of the Nara Inlet. Because there is no evidence of other mammal bones in these excavations, it can be asserted that oysters were the main source of protein. While some hunter-gatherer tribes might follow animal migrations for their sustenance, large permanent or semi-permanent communities could be established on a coast where a ready supply of oysters and other fish were always available.

Thus far only natural oyster beds have been discussed, but an important question is: when and where did humans begin to cultivate oysters? Some Russian scholars argue that as early

Whaleback shell midden along the Damariscotta River in Maine; the shells are over 2,000 years old.

On the Nara Inlet on Hook Islands in the Whitsunday National Forest, Queensland, Australia, are stylized oyster cave paintings by the Ngaro aboriginal people dating back thousands of years.

as 6,000 years ago oyster farming existed in southern Primorye on Boisman Bay in the Pacific, near modern Vladivostok. The Boisman excavation has produced a stupendous find: 98.5 per cent of the shells have been identified as *Crassostrea gigas* (the Pacific oyster), the middens of which have been radiocarbon-dated to 6,500 years ago, and 85 per cent of these shells were from oysters that were more than two years old. This high percentage implies that other, less desirable species were culled and that those which remained were left to grow to a larger, more appetizing size. The debate will continue, but in an era when food was an uncertainty, it is feasible that Stone Age man understood the oyster well enough to sort small from large and wait patiently before feasting.

The Civilized Oyster

The earliest example of oyster consumption within an ancient civilization was made apparent when Heinrich Schliemann undertook the excavation in 1876 of Hissarlik – now presumed to be the ancient site of Troy – in modern Turkey. No one could have suspected that he would discover oyster shells among all five settlements. There was a large number of unopened oyster shells in the first tomb, perhaps as food left for the deceased, or for the departed to offer to the gods in the afterlife. Oyster-shell amulets were found in excavations of the Egyptian Middle Kingdom (2000 BC to 1750 BC) and were thought to promote health, as the words for 'shell' and 'healthy' sound similar. Legend has it that Cleopatra once wagered with Mark Antony that she could stage the most elaborate and expensive dinner party ever conceived. In her attempt to promote Egypt's wealth and superiority, Cleopatra removed her large pearl earrings and crushed one of the pearls, dissolving it in her goblet of wine. Drinking the contents, she offered Antony the matching pearl. He declined and conceded the bet. According to Pliny, the two pearls were estimated to be valued at 60 million sesterces (approximately £2 million or $2.4 million today).

The ancient Greek philosopher Plato (428–348 BC) used oysters as a demeaning metaphor in his treatise *Timaeus*, which concerned the concept of the transmigration of souls. Here it is said that men who have lived effeminately will be changed into women, those who have frittered away their life will be changed into birds and those who have given no thought to philosophy will become beasts of burden. Those ignoble beings who lived without considering philosophical questions will be relegated to having their souls transmigrated into oysters. Aristotle (384–322 BC) was the first to document the habits and virtues of oysters, in his *History of Animals*. Although he obviously observed them carefully, almost all his conclusions were horrifically wrong: he believed that oysters were spontaneously generated from water and mud and were possibly not even living creatures.

Gastronomically, oysters began to appear in the earliest known cookbooks in the third-century AD Greek *Deipnos-ophistae* and the Roman cookbook *Apicius* (compiled in the late fourth or early fifth century, but attributed to a gourmet who lived in the first century). Larensius, a wealthy Roman scholar, could be considered the world's earliest food writer. His fifteen-book series entitled the *Deipnosophistae* – literally translated as 'The Dinner Experts' – was thought superficially to be nothing other than a description of parties, but includes analysis of society, sexual mores and gossip, as well as food and wine. On the subject of oysters, he wrote:

> Oysters are reproduced in rivers, lagoons and the sea. But sea oysters are the best, when a lagoon or a river is near. For then they have a good liquor, and are larger and sweeter. Those which are found on beaches or rocks and are untouched by slime or fresh water are small, tough and biting to the tongue. The spring shell-fish, and those which come at the beginning of summer, are superior, being plump and having a sea flavour mixed with sweetness; they are wholesome and digestible. Cooked with mallow or sorrel or fish, or even alone, they are nourishing and good for the bowels.

Where did all these oysters that the Romans and Greeks love so much come from? For the Greeks, it was easy as all their major cities were built very close to the ocean. There is speculation that the Greeks may be tied with the Chinese for being the first to cultivate the oyster. Greek fishermen could see that baby oysters would attach themselves to pieces of pottery that had been discarded into the waters. Since they wanted to make it easier to get the adult oyster later, these shards with small, attached oysters were moved to more accessible locations near the coastline. The oyster had found an acceptable substrate or cultch (the pottery shard) on which were attached baby oysters (spat) that were moved to other regions (called 'bedding') until large enough to eat. The word 'ostracize' – now meaning 'to exclude someone' – is of Greek origin and is related to the oyster. In ancient Greece a yearly popular vote was held to banish a citizen (usually someone who was unpopular or who had gained too much power) for five or ten years. These votes took place by carving the particular person's name on a pottery shard called an *ostrakon*, which had an oyster-like shape.

Oyster acquisition was more complex for the Romans, whose capital was inland and whose territorial conquests eventually extended hundreds of miles up the Danube and to the deserts of North Africa. The Pyrrhic and Punic wars (280–146 BC) brought Roman armies down the Italian Peninsula to the Adriatic Sea and the Mediterranean coastline, where they discovered oysters. Emperor Tiberius is reputed to have feasted on and sustained his troops with the oysters found in the Bay of Mali Ston, now in modern-day Croatia. At the time, it was the Roman province of Illyricum. When the Romans reached and conquered the peoples along the Atlantic coastline of Brittany (the coasts of England and France), they also discovered the European oyster (*Ostrea edulis*). At low tide, tens of thousands of oysters were exposed on the tide-flats and many soldiers stationed along the northern European territories would stop their fighting long enough to pick oysters. Inland excavation of ancient Roman guard station sites in

Germany and Switzerland backs up the hypothesis that the oysters were packed in snow for hauling to these distant locales. Other accounts have the oysters being shipped via merchant vessels to the armies heading inland. It was Apicius who figured out a way to pack fresh oysters for transport, sending the much-loved shellfish to the emperor Trajan on the Mesopotamia campaign of AD 115. Even then, the oyster was a food of excess with reports of Seneca consuming a thousand oysters a week and the Roman emperor Vitellius eating a thousand oysters in one sitting.

Regardless of which civilization originated oyster cultivation, the first documentation of the feat goes to the Roman scientist Pliny the Elder (AD 23–79), in his *Natural History*:

> Sergius Orata was the first man to invent oyster ponds,
> on the Gulf of Baiae in the time of the orator L. Crassus,
> before the Marsic war; his motive was not gluttony but
> avarice, and he earned great income for his cleverness.
> (Book IX, 168)

What Orata had done was fairly innovative. Witnessing the popularity of imported oysters, Orata figured out how to create an artificial oyster bed in Lucrinus (Lucrine Lake) in Campania with the construction of dams and channels that would protect the oysters from ocean tides. He worked out new breeding techniques by placing twigs around mature, spawning oysters in order to catch the new spat that was floating about, then transported the babies to the newly created oyster beds. The Roman civil engineer and author Vitruvius credits Orata with the invention of the hypocaust – or under-floor heating – which enabled him to keep the oysters from dying during the cold winters. There is some debate over whether Orata was really the inventor, but it is known that he constructed a large suspended water basin under which existed a *praeferium* (fireplace). The ductwork system used to pipe warm water to the oyster beds to keep them from freezing was quickly repurposed as public baths using circulated hot water; these *balneae pensiles* began appearing all over the Roman Empire.

Lucius Crassus, a famed orator, defended Orata in a lawsuit against a Roman tax farmer, Consilius, over a dispute on the public resource of the Lucrine Lake. From the court records, we have Crassus' account of the opulence of oysters in Orata's feasts:

> Not far from these oyster beds rose a palace in which the wealthy Roman used to assemble his choicest friends, and feast with them the whole day and night. Oysters occupied the place of honour on the table of Sergius Orata; at every feast, thousands of them were consumed. Satiated, but not yet satisfied, these gourmets were in the habit of adjourning into an adjoining room, where they relieved the stomach of its load by artificial means, and then returned to indulge again their appetite with a fresh supply of oysters.

Many pieces of art attest to the Romans' love of oysters and one wonderful example is the Populonia Bottle, a delicate green bottle that measures 18.4 cm (7.2 in.) high and 12.3 cm (4.8 in.) around, currently in the Corning Museum of Glass in New York. That it still exists is astonishing, and the image on the bottle is very telling. While Roman glassmakers usually polished their cut decorations, this bottle is heavily incised with diagrams which depict the construction of pylons from which ropes dangle with sacks full of oysters, and the explanatory word *OSTRIARIA*. This verifies aquafarming techniques

The Populonia Bottle, a delicate green bottle with oyster-farm diagrams and the explanatory word *OSTRIARIA*, which depicts the construction on pylons from which ropes dangle with sacks full of oysters.

and it is easy to see the mechanisms by which the oysters can be cleaned, sorted and culled.

The ancient Roman aristocracy prided themselves on being connoisseurs, ostentatiously comparing different breeds of oyster. Gaius Licinius Mucianus, a first-century Roman general, statesman and writer, rhapsodized on the oysters found at Cyzicus, a town in Asia Minor, on the shores of the Sea of Marmara (what is now Turkey). He described the bivalves there as larger than those of Lucrinus, fresher than those of the British coasts, sweeter than those of Medulae (the district in the vicinity of Bordeaux, now called Medoc), tastier than those of Ephesus, more plump than those of Lucus, less slimy than those of Coryphas, more delicate than those of Istria and whiter than those of Circeii. Testament to the oyster cult in ancient Rome is the number of penned treatises on a mere consumable: Horace, Cicero, Seneca, Martial, Juvenal and more all had something to say about the oyster. In Juvenal's satires, he comments on a fellow citizen: 'So skilled in eating was Montanus, that at the first bite of an oyster, he could tell where they were taken.'

The Greeks were the physicians of the ancient era and Mnesitheus, a fourth-century BC Greek physician, in his treatise on *Comestibles* warns:

> Oysters, and cockles, and mussels, and similar things are not very digestible in their meat, because of a sort of saline moisture which there is in them, on which account, when eaten raw, they produce an effect on the bowels by reason of their saltiness. But when boiled they get rid of all, or at all events of most, of their saltiness, which they infuse into the water which boils them. On which account, the water in which any of the oyster tribe are boiled is very apt to have a strong effect in disordering

the bowels. But the meat of the oysters, when boiled, makes a great noise when it has been deprived of its moisture. But roasted oysters, when any one roasts them cleverly, are very free from any sort of inconvenience; for all the evil properties are removed by fire; on which account they are not indigestible as raw ones, and they have all the moisture which is originally contained in them dried up; and it is the moisture which has too great effect in relaxing the bowels. But every oyster supplies a moist and somewhat indigestible kind of nourishment, and they are not at all good as diuretics.

I doubt that most Romans believed this, considering the number of raw oysters consumed. We won't hear much about oysters again in Europe until the Middle Ages. Instead, the glory of the oyster rises in the East.

3
Oysters in Asia

While Western civilization was experiencing its rise and fall, the cult of the oyster was expanding in the Far East, both for the acquisition of pearls and for dining purposes. We know the ancient Greeks and Romans were practising aquafarming, but a politician named Fan Li penned the earliest-known Chinese document on the subject, *Yang Yu Ching* (Treatise on Fish Breeding), in 475 BC. Oyster farming had also been recorded during the Han Dynasty (206 BC–AD 220). During the Tang Dynasty (AD 618–907), every sort of oyster was sought along the extensive coasts of that empire. Charles Benn, in his book *The Golden Age of China*, discusses the dining habits of the imperial family, who 'enjoyed eating cooked jellyfish with cinnamon, Sichuan pepper, cardamom, and ginger, as well as oysters with wine'. In the fourth year of K'ai Yuan, AD 716, natural pearls were found in the waters of Tolo Harbour – about 23 km (14 mi.) north of Hong Kong. Sadly, the discovery of those pearls begat a rather morbid practice of oyster collection: a diver was weighted with heavy stones and lowered over the side of a *sampan* (a small fishing skiff) by a rope. When his colleagues thought he had been under the water long enough, he and his bounty were hauled up. The mortality rate of these oyster divers was very high and it is said that the emperor Wen-tsung (809–840) was so enamoured with oysters that the fishermen were compelled to supply their monarch with no recompense or consideration of the loss of life.

There is a legend, however, that an exceptionally large oyster was presented to the emperor, but no one was able to open the monstrosity. In disgust, the monarch was about to throw the oyster away when it opened of its own accord, revealing a miraculous image of Kuan Yin, the Goddess of Mercy. The emperor was so overwhelmed that he ordered the oyster be preserved in a gold-lined sandalwood box as he sent for a local oracle to interpret the image. The Buddhist oracle Wei Cheng advised, 'The Pusa Kuan Yin has chosen this means of inclining your majesty's mind to benevolence and clemency and of filling your heart with pity for your oppressed people.' The emperor abolished the forced levy of oysters, but several hundred years later, around 964, the Mongols revived the practice, enslaving the Nam Hoi Yan (the Tanka boat people), an ethnic group from southern China and Vietnam known for living on junks and surviving on the water. The oyster fishing methods were the same as before and the death rate was as high as ever, provoking violent protests until a local elder, Chang Wei-yin, managed to persuade those in power to reconsider. By imperial order, the oyster-diving practice was abandoned. The harvesting of oysters continued, however, with the Ming Dynasty in 1374. After the pearls had been gathered or the oysters had been eaten, the poor would burn the shells to make lime. It did not take long to determine that the particular area in the harbour had been overfarmed and new, fresh beds were developed near Leizhou Bay, about 500 km (310 mi.) west of Hong Kong. While we can only speculate on all the locations where oysters were found in ancient China, today there are more than twenty regions in China where oysters are farmed, ranging from Bohai to the South China Sea.

Traditional Chinese Medicine (TCM) is based on Taoist philosophies which assert that humans are part of nature and need to remain in harmony with nature. These beliefs ascribe a yin-yang balance to all that governs life in the universe, with yin being dark, cold, wet and feminine, while yang is light, warm, dry, male and energetic. In this regard, the oyster is considered 'too cold' and therefore unhealthy to consume in its raw form. Besides the burning for lime, the oyster shells, known as *mu li*, have been a medicinal supplement for centuries. Once ground to a powder they are considered to have salty and cooling properties which are associated with the liver and kidneys and are known to calm the 'spirits' – that is, palpitations, anxiety, restlessness and insomnia.

A dried, salted oyster is a wholesale commodity as well as being considerably easier to transport than an oyster that is whole and in its shell. Oysters are sold in two states, 'dried

In China, oysters are dried on racks in the sun at the Lau Fau Shan fish market and sold in bulk.

raw' and 'dried cooked', the latter being the famous oyster sauce, a thick, viscous and dark-brown liquid that is sweet and smoky, beefy and earthy – full of umami and a hint of mystery. Starting with hundreds of pounds of raw oyster meat, the sauce is created by salting, washing and boiling the oysters. Once this is drained and strained, fresh oysters are added and the process is started again. Care is taken to assure the sauce does not get too thick with the addition of fresh water until it reaches the proper consistency, when it is cooled in large clay vats and then strained into pottery jars. Sealed, these jars can weigh up to 22 kg (50 lb) and the contents are aged for a year or longer. The oysters that have been strained out are considered the 'cooked oysters', which can now be dried, as described by Frederick Simoons in his excellent book *Food in China* (1990):

first for five or six hours in the sun, then for another twelve hours in the shade. Then they were coated with peanut oil to make them glossy, and marketed in large bamboo baskets. Such dried cooked oysters, which keep for about a week, were less tasty and much less expensive than the dried raw oysters, which were usually sold retail in bottles.

An essential condiment in Chinese and Vietnamese cooking, oyster sauce is commonly used in stir-fried noodles, chow mein and popular dishes such as beef and broccoli. There exists some debate on the addition of other ingredients like soy sauce, brine or seasonings. The inventor of oyster sauce, it has been claimed, was Lee Kam Sheung, from the Nam Shui Village in Guangdong, in 1888. Sheung made his living running a small eatery that sold cooked oysters and he claimed that

One day, [he] was cooking oysters as usual, but lost track of time until he smelt a strong aroma. Lifting the lid of the pot, he noticed that the normally clear oyster soup had turned into a thick, brownish sauce which astonished him with the most fragrant smell and unique, delicious taste.

Sheung's story is probably folklore, as there is documentation of the sauce's prior existence, as indicated in an article of 1875 in *China Review*, 'Ostriculture in China', which states, 'the oyster sauce Hau Yeou is rather good and could be used in other countries.' Another chef, Lǐ Jǐnshàng, is also credited with having invented the oyster sauce in Nanshui, Zhugahi, in 1888. Sheung was the first to capitalize on the creation of a good recipe, forming the Lee Kum Kee company to bottle and distribute the sauce on a large scale, thereby creating an empire that is still going strong today.

Though the Chinese were the first recorded society in Asia to extensively process oysters, other cultures also adopted the practice. The Japanese first cultivated the oyster in the sixteenth century around Hiroshima, where Manila clams were also being farmed. Bamboo stalks known as *shibi* were used to create enclosures in the shallow waters for the clams, but those stalks became the cultch to which wild baby oysters would attach. The Japanese fishermen quickly learned that the oysters were more valuable than the clams and, in a technique that is still used today, started dangling ropes to catch the spat – now known as the hanging-culture method of cultivation. With this development, strings of oysters are hung in the water from rafts or racks until harvest (the same technique depicted on the Roman bottle discussed in Chapter Two).

Two differing methods to the hanging-culture procedure exist. In southern Japan, one-month-old seed oysters are

Just a few of the dozens of different oyster sauces available on the market today.

moved to rafts and can be harvested for commercial market after one year. This method involves minimal labour, as the oysters have little time to attach themselves to other material and are protected from predators. In northern Japan, predominantly in Miyagi prefecture, a two-year culture is the norm. There, after the seed has been set, the strings are draped over racks – above the water – during each tide cycle. The elevation is necessary due to the 'oyster drill', a predator shell which thrives in the muddy depths and bores its way into the oyster. The elevated oysters grow all summer causing the shells to harden, resulting in substantial growth and longer survival rates. By the autumn, these oysters are transferred to rafts and continue to grow until the following year. With this two-year culture, if the water is very deep, longer lines of string can be used. This method utilizes more space as the columns of rope are not limited by depth, and it therefore allows for the industry to grow.

In Japan, long before the cultivation of oysters, girls and women known as *ama* were renowned for their ability to dive deep and gather pearls from wild oysters at the sea bottom. Many Japanese woodcuts of the eighteenth and nineteenth centuries were devoted to the depiction of the beauty and allure of these women. The girls would wear only a small loin-cloth, *fundoshi*, and hair bandana, *tenugui*, baring their naked breasts. Many Western explorers may have believed they were spying on mermaids as the sound of the *ama-bui*, a whistle, was heard when the women surfaced from their depths.

The Hiroshima oysters in Japan gained a splendid reputation for pearls during the Edo period (1603–1868). These were traded over a large area, but little is documented about the consumption of their meat during this era. How Japan became a hero in the oyster industry had nothing to do with

Japanese *Chirimen-gami-e* (compressed thread paper); 18th-century image of an oyster seller.

Mikimoto pearl divers.

their pearls, but with the creation of two of the most famous oysters in culinary history: the Miyagi (*Crassostrea gigas*) and the Kumamoto (*Crassostrea sikamea*). In America, at the end of the nineteenth century, disease, overexploitation and extensive pollution of oyster beds on both the east and west coasts caused severely depleted availability of the bivalve. Up until the beginning of the twentieth century in America, oysters were a very inexpensive and accessible commodity, especially for the working poor, and one-third of American fisheries at that point had been farming the Atlantic and Olympia oysters. The Pacific coast farmers in California, Washington and Oregon had grown dependent upon East Coast shipments of oyster seed, but these shipments were becoming more expensive and increasingly scarce.

Through the intervention of Japanese and u.s. government researchers, starting in 1902 seed oysters from Japan were shipped first to Samish Bay and then other areas of Puget Sound in Washington state where new crops could be established. The first shipment to Willapa Bay in Washington occurred in 1904 and then in British Columbia around 1912. Coming from the Miyagi prefecture, many different species were attempted but the one that would save the dying American industry was *Crassostrea gigas* (that Pacific oyster now known as the Miyagi oyster). Because of its great adaptability to new environments, ultimately the Miyagi has almost replaced the native Olympia. It has seen successes in different habitats from as far south as southern California up into Canada. It has withstood and developed resistance to multiple diseases. Sadly, the seed shipments were put on hold during the Second World War but they restarted in 1945 thanks to General Douglas MacArthur. He assisted in ending the wartime embargo and requested 80,000 boxes of oyster seed from the Japanese government, mostly from the Matsushima islands in northeastern Japan. The oyster industry in Japan had suffered due to the war and Miyagi seed was limited, so the Japanese supplemented their order with thirty boxes of Kumamoto seed oysters (*C. sikamea*), sent firstly as a test. Since the 1860s Kumamotos had been farmed in Japan's Shiranui Sea, but their diminutive nature made them less desirable to the Japanese, who preferred larger, faster-growing oysters. Kumamotos only grow to about 5 cm (2 in.) across and take a full three years to mature. Their subtle, delicate flavour gained a strong following in the u.s. and became popular very quickly.

After the war, shipments resumed more regularly, with a complicated shipping process. First, seed – still hanging from wires – was brought in from the bay where the mostly women workers cut the strings, washed the shells and separated the clusters with a culling hammer. The spat was then packed into wooden *sake* boxes and carefully loaded onto the decks of boats that could accommodate more than two hundred boxes. The live oysters could not survive in the warm hull of a ship, so instead were placed on deck where the sailors could tend their cargo. Straw mats were thrown atop the boxes and watered twice a day during the oysters' two-week journey.

The boxes could not be stacked too high, lest the bottom oysters dry out. From the end of the Second World War until the 1970s, when the American industry was able to stand on its own, 100,000 cases of seed were shipped per year.

Fate has lent a hand to the survival of the Kumamoto. In 1956, in the Kumamoto prefecture in Japan, humans began experiencing horrible symptoms ultimately referred to as Minamata disease. The Chisso Corporation was guilty of dumping methylmercury into Minamata Bay and the Shiranui Sea from 1932 until 1968. This act poisoned all the shellfish and fish to the extent that many people and animals who had consumed food from those waters suffered symptoms including severe numbness to the extremities, loss of vision and damage to hearing and speech. Many children were born with severe defects. To date, almost 1,800 people have died, an entire town was poisoned and the local seafood industry was

The Kumamoto – one of the Japanese oysters that saved a worldwide industry – is favoured by new oyster eaters. It comes in a deep-cupped shell and is small in the mouth, with a mild brininess, a sweet flavour and a honeydew finish.

completely destroyed. The prized Kumamoto oyster can no longer be grown in the very region that gave birth to it.

The beneficial legacy of the Japanese propagation of seed was not limited to the Americas. Until the 1960s the coastal shores of Brittany and Normandy were famous for their Portuguese oyster (*C. angulata*) and their European flat oyster (*O. edulis*). In the 1960s a gill disease decimated most of the Portuguese oyster population, but another cupped oyster, the Pacific (*C. gigas*), was brought from Japan to help re-seed failing beds starting with the Bay of Marennes-Oléron. A decade later when 80 per cent of the European flat had been destroyed by parasites, it was experts from British Columbia who would save the day from their beds which had previously been restocked from the Japanese. *L'Operation Résur* was a twofold project that occurred between 1971 and 1975; first to create healthy sanctuaries and then to supply the oystermen with healthy *C. gigas* spat from Canadian waters. That very same Japanese spat that had saved the Canadians earlier in the century was now being placed in the Bays of Bourgneuf, Arcachon and Marennes-Oléron, as well as the areas around La Rochelle and Gironde. Today the French produce 1,500 tonnes of *O. edulis* and more than 130,000 tonnes of the cupped *C. gigas* annually – all thanks to the Japanese. Currently, Chinese and Japanese oyster production collectively accounts for more than 80 per cent of the world's total output, whereas a hundred years ago the largest global producer was the United States. Korea is also a huge producer of farmed oysters, producing more than 300,000 tonnes per year. However, it is the Japanese who became the true heroes, saving a worldwide dying oyster industry after the Second World War.

4
Oysters from the Middle Ages to the 1800s

When the Roman Empire fell in the fifth century AD, written documentation of oyster consumption throughout Europe stopped. Monks who kept literacy alive were more interested in doctrine than dining, so it is upon archaeologists we rely to verify oyster consumption throughout the world. In the 1980s three distinct archaeological excavations in Leicester, in the East Midlands of the UK, demonstrated that the European flat was being consumed from the first century into the fourth century and again from the 1100s to the 1500s. Changes in the management of these oyster beds were identifiable by the subtle differences in the strata. Oyster fossils from the earlier excavations were significantly larger, indicating that patient gourmets were willing to wait for the oysters to mature. Several centuries later, the oysters consumed were physically smaller as impatient diners would farm the oysters before they were able to grow as large as their older brethren. One reason may have been the decline in trade routes, as oysters were once gourmet treats for the wealthy Roman citizens and now only sustained local villagers.

The exception to the established pattern of Roman expansion occurred in Scandinavia, where middens dating from the Stone Age to the present confirm continuous consumption

Camulodunum, the Roman name for what is now Colchester in Essex, is probably the oldest British town and famous for its oysters – from the Roman era to the present day.

of oysters. In March 1878 the *Magazine of Natural History* published an article titled 'On the Geographical Distribution of the Common Oyster', by G. Winther, which placed oysters

> at Heligoland, on the western coast of Slesvig, in the Limfjord, the Aalbæk Bay in the Kattegat, and along the eastern shore of Jutland, as far as the fjord of Horsens, whilst on the coast of the Scandinavian peninsula oysters are found from a point south of Gothenborg along the Swedish and Norwegian coasts towards the bay of Christiania, and again on the south and west coast of Norway as far as the island of Tränen, near the polar circle.

Vikings sailed these waters in *karves*, smaller versions of their *knarrs*, the dragon-headed cargo ships. Both vessels were constructed for use in war and transportation, but the *karves* were agile enough to navigate the shallow, oyster-rich waters of the coastlines. As plentiful as the oysters were to the Vikings – and it is known that they *were* eaten – consuming them was considered cowardly and unmanly. During the seventh century, a militant warrior named Starkad criticized the legendary Swedish king Ingjald for frying and cooking his food as well as consuming oysters, all of which were considered unmanly or unworthy of a true Viking.

The period from the fifth to the eleventh century brought the rise and fall of the Anglo-Saxons in England and France. The last Saxon monarch, King Harold (1022–1066), so famously depicted on the Bayeux Tapestry, held as one of his possessions a manor named Moverons in the small fishing village of Brightlingsea, about 16 km (10 mi.) south of Colchester in Britain. Excavations of the Moverons quarry produced significant artefacts of Anglo-Saxon life, including bowls, loom weights and large quantities of oyster shells – enough to indicate that they were used as a food source. The importance of a fishery as an asset for a king is documented throughout the Domesday Book, ordered twenty years after the Battle of Hastings of 1066 by Harold's successor, William the Conqueror. The book's purpose was to categorize the country's holdings for tax purposes and to prepare the military against the threat of Danish invasion in 1085, but it has become an invaluable resource for historians for the breadth of information provided on the distribution of landed property. The town of Tollesbury, for example, lists 'fishery, 3 salthouses, 2 cobs, 10 cattle, 300 sheep'. Tollesbury, in the county of Essex, sits on the Blackwater estuary, a well-loved Roman oyster bed. A nearby Saxon/Norman church was built on the Roman site and it is one of many locations where oysters continue to be enjoyed to this day.

Medieval Europeans followed Catholic ideas imposing the concept of 'fish days', on which the flesh of animals and birds could not be consumed. Early on, meatless days were Wednesdays, Fridays and Saturdays, as well as Advent, Lent and numerous other holy days. This practice helped to grow a global fishing industry. Medieval folklore forbade the mixing of fish and fowl in the same meal, but by the 1700s oyster stuffing appeared with Saturday feasts of roast capon or duck. An early medieval mention of oysters appears in the *Exeter Book*, an Anglo-Saxon collection of riddles published in 1072:

> The sea fed me; the water-helm was over me
> And waves covered me, close to the ground
> I was footless. Often toward the water
> I opened my mouth. Now people will
> Eat my meat. They want not my skin
> When they rip my hide with the point of a knife
> Then they eat me uncooked.

For the first time since Apicius, oysters appeared in a cookbook: *The Forme of Cury* (1390), written by the master chefs of King Richard II. This famous medieval cookbook presents oysters in both sweet and savoury recipes, such as boiling shucked oysters in wine and their own liquor, then adding either sugar and spices or onions and herbs. This demand for oysters revived a long-dormant trade between the coasts and inland cities as transportation of oysters began anew. Inland residents received their shipments in barrels of

An oyster from the medieval manuscript of Jacob van Maerlant's *Der naturen bloeme* (c. 1350).

Designed by Johannes Stradanus around 1550, this 1613 print shows oyster fishing; from a rowing boat oysters are fished up with nets and brought to shore for processing.

seawater, allowing the oysters to stay alive for two to three weeks. Given that roads were primitive and oxcarts slow, oysters were still not available very far from any coastal hamlet, but it was a step towards expanding oyster consumption.

The first oyster festival in the world was established when Edward II, king of England from 1312 to 1327, decreed that the St Denys Fair in Colchester – first held in September 1318 – be moved to coincide with the beginning of oyster season at the end of October. To this day, the Colchester Medieval Festival and Oyster Fayre Market is one of the largest and most well-attended oyster celebrations in the world. By looking at *The Forme of Cury*, we can speculate how the general populace of Britain cooked their oysters, but ample documentation suggests their kings favoured oysters raw and Henry IV (1367–1413) regularly downed four hundred in one sitting as a precursor to his main meal. The discovery in 2014 of Richard III's (1452–1485) final resting place under what is now a car park in Leicester has allowed for an unprecedented scientific analysis of a monarch's remains. The levels of isotopes of oxygen, strontium, nitrogen and carbon indicate that Richard had a very rich diet that included peacocks, herons, swans, wine and oysters – lots and lots of oysters – which can be attributed to the fact that religious observances required a meat-free diet for up to one-third of the year.

The French monarchs from medieval to Renaissance times – all named Louis – were just as obsessed with oysters as their British counterparts. Louis IV (920–954), taken to England as a child by his mother, Eadgifu, developed a taste for the English oyster – so much so that when he was captured and imprisoned for a year in Normandy by Hugues le Grand, Louis requested and received a regular ration of oysters. Louis IX (1214–1270), concerned with intellectual matters, ordered the doctors of the Sorbonne to dine on a feast of oysters at least once a year. The famous Sun King, Louis XIV (1638–1715), had an absolute monarchy which lasted for 72 years with nary a monarch to match his grandeur, opulence or gluttony. His love of oysters was so intense that a daily supply arrived from the French coasts of Cancale, regardless of which palace the king was inhabiting, for every meal began with six dozen iced, raw oysters. If the weather was warm or there was a hint of spoilage, his physicians would order the oysters to be cooked.

The belief that oysters should be consumed only during a month with an 'r' in its spelling is first documented in a Leonine proverb from the Middle Ages: *mensibus erratis vos ostrea manducatis* 'in the R'd months you may your oysters eat.' Where this idea originated from cannot be pinpointed, but James I's (1566–1625) physician, William Butler (1535–1618), is reputed to have been among the first to utter the warning.

The first documentation in print is in an inconsequential book known as *Dyets Dry Dinner*. Printed in 1599 and written by Henry Buttes (d. 1632), it gives an account of eight different dinner courses (fruits, herbs, flesh, fish, white meat, spice, sauce and tobacco), coupled with suggested related table-talk. It is dedicated to Miss Lady Anne Bacon and one can assume Dr Buttes was attempting to seduce the young lady with a good meal. On oysters he advises against consuming them in months with an 'r' in the name, erroneously assumes that oysters grow upon the bottoms of large vessels, and believes they are hard to digest and cause phlegm and constipation. Convinced that raw oysters have a 'cold nature', he offers recipes to transform them into something more appealing. Dr Buttes also attempts to play down the then-held belief that an oyster incites sexual desire, probably to convince the young lady of his noble intentions.

Oysters were now food for the common folk. Early printed cookbooks such as Sir Hugh Plat's *Delightes for Ladies* (1602) instructed housewives 'how to barrel up oysters, so as they shall last for sixe moneths sweet and good, and in their natural taste'. Consumed all over the European continent, the most prized oysters were believed to come from the British Isles. *England as Seen by the Foreigners in the Days of Elizabeth and James I*, composed from journals of the Duke of Würtemberg from 1592 and 1610 (but not published until 1865 by W. B. Rye), contain numerous comments on British oysters, including those of Jacob Rathgeb from Switzerland, who remarked on their fine quality: 'Oysters are in great plenty, and are better and larger than in Italy.' Laws regarding the governance and harvesting of oysters were cited in 1577, prohibiting the dredging of oyster beds at the mouth of the Medway River between Easter and Lammas (mid-April until 1 August).

Das Kochbuch der Sabina Welserin, a German cookbook of 1533, may contain the first recipe for simple grilling:

> Wash the Oysters very clean and open them, salt and pepper them and lay them on the grill in the half shells in which you have found them. And pour butter on them, that is, in the shells, and let them roast in a good heat as long as one roasts eggs. Then bring them warm to the table, so that the butter remains in them.

The first oyster pie recipe is found in the French *Ouverture de cuisine* (1604), by Master Lancelot de Casteau. Italian cookbooks, Cristoforo di Messisbugo's *Libro nuovo nel qua si insegna a far d'ogni sorte di vivanda* (1564) and Bartolomeo Scappi's *Opera dell'arte del cucinare* (1570), are filled with numerous illustrations showing large platters of oysters, but offer little advice regarding preparation. Modern scientific evidence suggests the *C. angulata* genus (the Portuguese oyster) originated

Osias Beert, *Dishes with Oysters, Fruit and Wine*, 1620s.

Jean-François de Troy, *The Oyster Lunch*, 1735. A raucous affair with oysters still to be eaten on the table and the floor littered with shells.

in Taiwan or the waters of northern China and arrived on European shores via the trade vessels of explorers like Vasco da Gama (1460s–1524), who established the route from Europe to the Indian Ocean via the Cape of Good Hope. What started off as the profitable eastern spice trade for the Portuguese to the European continent unwittingly brought the transplant of *C. angulata* to the French estuaries where they thrived in brackish waters. Soon, the French were happily dining on Portuguese oysters thanks to these trading vessels offering exotic spices.

Oysters made a grand entrance into the visual arts during the fifteenth century, most prevalently in Flemish still-life paintings, where a closed oyster displayed in proximity to a woman would symbolize virtue or virginity, while an opened oyster alluded to libidinous behaviour. In *The Senses, Taste, Hearing and Touch* (*c.* 1620) by Jan Brueghel the Elder, a female figure is sitting alone at a table that is set with an overflowing, bounteous feast of oysters, fruit, wine, crayfish and quail. Her exposed bosom near a large quantity of opened oysters alludes to an ecstatic, wanton state. That she, herself, is plunging a fork into an oyster implies that she is the sexual instigator.

By the mid-1600s oysters were everyday fare, readily and inexpensively available from street vendors at almost any time, day or night. We have the noted British diarist Samuel Pepys (1633–1703) to thank for the best record of the common man's dining habits, as he and his contemporaries could dine upon oysters from street vendors, in local taverns while discussing politics or in his home after ordering a barrelful of oysters from a local stall. Social status could be displayed to dinner guests with a fancy preparation of larger oysters (signifying they were shipped in), but smaller offerings were a common street food. Besides the barrel, oysters also came in 'bushels' or 'pecks'. There are four pecks in a bushel and a bushel is about one hundred oysters. Barrels of oysters came two ways: fresh or pickled. In Pepys's time, these small barrels would range from 18 cm (7 in.) to 30 cm (12 in.) high. First soaked in salt water, the barrels were then filled with fresh oysters for transit, keeping the oysters alive this way for several days. These barrels cost two to three shillings apiece and

could contain anywhere from fifteen to thirty oysters. For a
dinner of 13 January 1663, Pepys wrote: 'my poor wife had to
rise at five in the morning to go grocery shopping for a meal
that included oysters, a hash of rabbit and lamb, a rare chine
of beef, a great dish of roasted fowle, and a tart, fruit, and
cheese.' Eating them for breakfast on 21 May 1660, Pepys
noted, 'So into my naked bed and slept 'till 9 o'clock and then
John Goods waked me, and by the captain's boy brought me
four barrels of Mallows oysters.' Pepys refers to Mallows oysters, Colchester oysters and some that were brought up from
the estuary of the Thames.

Much has been made of Dr Samuel Johnson's (1709–
1784) cat, about whom James Boswell wrote in *The Life of
Samuel Johnson* (1799), 'I never shall forget the indulgence with
which he treated Hodge, his cat: for whom he himself used

to go out and buy oysters, lest the servants having that trouble should take a dislike to the poor creature.' Pickled oysters were available from any street vendor, or an industrious housewife could be taught how to pickle by Edward Kidder in his 1720 book *Receipts of Pastry and Cookery*:

> Take a qt. of large oysters in the full of the moon per-boyld in their own liquor for the pickle take a liquor a pt. of white wine & vinegar mace pepper & salt boyle & scum it when cold keep the oysters in this pickle.

From the housewife to the glutton, oyster love knows no bounds. Alexandre-Balthazar-Laurent Grimod de La Reynière (1758–1837) was a young lawyer and occasional theatre critic when he established himself as the world's first restaurant critic and ostensible food writer. Belonging to a well-heeled tasting society, he penned the eight-volume *Almanach des Gourmands* (1803–1812), which expounds,

> Oysters are the usual opening to a winter breakfast – indeed they are almost indispensable. But this is often a dear introduction through the indiscretion of guests who generally pride themselves on packing them by the hundred in their vainglorious stomachs. Insipid pleasure, which brings no real enjoyment, and often embarrasses the estimable host. It is proved by experience that, beyond five- or six-dozen, oysters certainly cease to be enjoyable.

Oysters that were worth stuffing in one's stomach were equally worth stealing. In 1791 an Act of Parliament in Great Britain passed an ordinance against pilfering, 'That if any person shall steal any oyster or oyster-brood from any

Marchande d'huitres des Environs
de la Rochelle.

From the mid-1600s to the turn of the last century, vendors known as 'criers' would wander the streets of London, Paris and New York to hawk their wares. Samuel Pepys acquired many oysters from sellers such as these.

oyster-bed . . . every such offender shall be deemed guilty of larceny, and being convicted thereof shall be punished accordingly.' The Act goes on to specify that it is a misdemeanour even to attempt to dredge another's oyster bed, regardless of whether any oysters are absconded with or not, and that the guilty be subjected to a fine of £20 or imprisonment, not to exceed three calendar months.

By the end of the eighteenth century, oysters were so plentiful and cheap that a gentleman could not force his household staff to eat them. Charles Dickens wrote in 1837: 'Poverty and oysters always seem to go together.' Dickens's wife, Catherine, published her own cookbook, *What Shall We Have for Dinner?*, under the pseudonym Lady Maria Clutterbuck in 1852, offering several recipes for oysters, including a favourite of her husband's: leg of lamb stuffed with oysters. It might seem that the bivalve's popularity was at a peak, but – surprisingly – the golden age of oyster eating was yet to come.

5
Oysters in the New World: America and Australia

The Age of Discovery was marked by fifteenth-century exploration: of the African coast by the Portuguese, the establishment of transatlantic routes to America by the Spanish, and the discovery of what was then known as *Terra Australis Ignota* (the unknown land of the south) by the Dutch. Granted, five centuries before this the Scandinavian Vikings had been exploring many of these destinations, but all this new travel led to worldwide oyster discoveries and consumption. European settlers began establishing colonies where oysters were most prevalent: on the shell-laden shores of New Brunswick in Canada, in the mollusc-heavy harbours of New York, all along the New England coastline, further south in America towards the Carolinas, and in the bountiful bays of Australia and New Zealand. The Dutch navigator Willem Janszoon is credited with being the first European to see the coast of Australia, arriving on the western shore of what is now Cape York in Queensland in 1606. He would call the land *Nieuw Holland*, where the indigenous Aborigines had been dining heartily on the Sydney rock oyster (*Saccostrea glomerata*, previously known as *S. commercialis*) and other, lesser-known oysters. The middens were tremendous; some were as large as 640 km (400 mi.) long and 6 km (4 mi.) high in New South Wales and

The shell midden at Spanish Mount, Edisto State Park, South Carolina.

southern Queensland, indicating thousands of years of oyster consumption.

In 1609, just a few years later, the Dutch sailed into America's Upper New York Bay and discovered a harbour full – at that time – of half the world's supply of oysters. Just below the Hudson River were 900 square km (350 sq. mi.) of oyster beds. These newly arriving Dutch immigrants would name the two islands in the New York harbour where oysters could be had: Great Oyster Island (now known as Liberty Island) and Little Oyster Island (now Ellis Island). Chartered by the Vereenigde Oostindische Compagnie (Dutch East India Company), numerous expeditions led to the establishment of 'New Netherland' – lands from the Chesapeake Bay and the Susquehanna River in the south and west, to Narragansett Bay and the Providence and Blackstone Rivers in the east, to the St Lawrence River in the north, all full of oysters. This area was inhabited by the indigenous Lenape population (also known as the Delaware Indians), who were already feasting on *Crassostrea virginica*, the Atlantic oyster.

Extensive middens of the Catawba and Yemassee peoples who lived in the Carolinas attest to the oyster's prominence and endurance in their native diet. *Chesapeake* means 'great shellfish bay', or *K'che-se-piak* in the language of the Algonquian peoples, also known as the Powhatan, or Virginia Indians. In 1612 an English settler to America, William Strachey, wrote of the oysters found in the Chesapeake:

> Oysters there be in whole bancks and beds, and those of the best I have seene some thirteen inches long. The savages use to boyle oysters and mussels together, and with the broath they make a good spoone meat, thickened with the flower of their wheat; an yt is a great thrit and husbandry with them to hang the oysters upon strings (being shaul and dried) in the smoake, thereby to preserve them all the yeare.

By the winter of 1620 British pilgrims were arriving in Provincetown on the tip of Cape Cod, either escaping religious persecution or to follow Strachey's lead for a good oyster. Within fifty years of the start of the 1600s, most of

America's East Coast territories were becoming colonized. In 1664, after a series of naval skirmishes during the Second Anglo-Dutch War, the Dutch lost their stronghold of 'New Netherland' and the lands were renamed Long Island and Brooklyn. New Amsterdam became New York and oyster consumption was thriving. Seventeenth-century recipes instructed diners to consume oysters raw or in stews or pottages, as well as in 'pyes', loaves and stuffings for the newly discovered and much-loved turkey.

Samuel Pepys told us of the availability of oysters via street vendors in London, and the newly transplanted European settlers were accustomed to such easy accessibility. This tradition continued in the Americas, specifically in New York City, where the oysters were not as physically easy to obtain. Along the shallower estuaries of New England, when the tide went out, it was very easy for any person to go and pick oysters. This was a similar practice to one Europeans had known in England, France and the Netherlands. In New York, the Lenape had taught the Dutch how to manage small skiffs and scrape up the oysters with tongs. For the colonists, these new American oysters were very different from the European oysters they had known so well. European flat oysters (*Ostrea edulis*) are known for their large, flat shells and bold, gamey taste. Atlantic oysters (*Crassostrea virginica*) are brinier, brighter and bigger. There were also many, many more of them.

In 1701 Francis Louis Michel was visiting the Chesapeake from Switzerland and observed that

> The abundance of oysters is incredible. There are whole banks of them so that the ships must avoid them . . . They surpass those in England by far in size, indeed, they are four times as large. I often cut them in two, before I could put them into my mouth.

North America was such a land of excess that by the beginning of the 1700s the oyster became exportable. For long voyages to the West Indies or southern Europe they were pickled. The British were still continuing their exploration of the globe, entering the South Pacific where the Dutch had colonized New Holland. Captain James Cook's HMS *Endeavour* arrived in Australia's Botany Bay in 1770, and the landing there produced a first-hand account of the oyster population:

> On the banks of land and mud there are great quantities of oysters, muscles, cockles and other shell fish, which seem to be the principal subsistence of the inhabitants, who go into shoal [shallow] water with their little canoes, and pick them out with their hands. It was not observed that they eat any of these shell fish raw, nor do they always

Map of New Netherland, now New Jersey, New York and Delaware, *c.* 1650.

go on shore to dress them, for they have frequently fires
in their canoes for that purpose.

Following America's transformation into a self-governing
country after the War of Independence (1775–83), reports of
the Founding Fathers enjoying oysters abounded. George
Washington's cash accounts at Mount Vernon document the
purchase of many bushels and barrels. A famous anecdote
involves Benjamin Franklin and illustrates the general difficulty of travelling great distances by horse on very muddy
roads in poor weather. After many hours of harsh riding,
Franklin arrived at a Rhode Island inn, hopeful of rest and
warmth by a fire. Seeing too many other travellers with the
same idea, and that there was no place to sit, he called loudly
to a servant, 'Boy, take a quart of oysters out to my horse!'
Incredulous that a horse would enjoy oysters, many of the
other travellers followed the boy outside to witness the

Emanuel Phillips Fox's 1902 oil painting depicts the first contact with
Captain James Cook and crew on the shores of the Kurnell Peninsula,
New South Wales.

David Rijckaert was just one of the many 17th-century Flemish Baroque painters to utilize oysters in their still-life paintings.

spectacle, thereby freeing up space by the fireplace for the weary Franklin. No account is given of what the horse thought of the oysters.

After the war's end, America set about exploring its own lands west of the Mississippi. Lewis and Clark began their 1803 Corps of Discovery Expedition across the western interior of the United States to the safe shelter of Puget Sound on the western coast, where they feasted on a seemingly inexhaustible supply of giant salmon and incredibly small oysters, the Olympia oyster, *Ostrea lurida*. 'When the tide goes out, the table is set' is a traditional saying of the Tlingit tribe of British Columbia and illustrates the abundance of the bounty offered up by the sea. Washington Irving (1783–1859) waxed poetic about oysters as an obsession in his *History of New York* (1809):

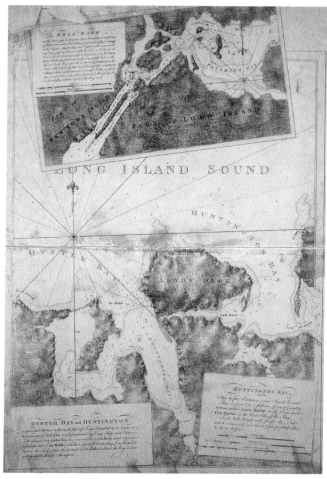

A detail from a navigational map dated 1873 instructs sailors how to enter Oyster Bay from Long Island Sound, separating New York from Connecticut: 'The Channel . . . lies over towards Loyds [sic] Neck until you are passed the tail of the Middle, (which is a sand flat extending from Hog Isle towards the Neck within the distance of 180 fathoms) thence the Bay is clear with good Anchorage throughout.'

In Wellfleet, Massachusetts, *c.* 1900, small shanties were built along the coast to work the nearby oyster beds. You can see the remains of the oyster shells that are stacked nearby after being shucked.

> Ever since the council-dinner of Oloffe the Dreamer at the founding of New Amsterdam, at which banquet the oyster figured so conspicuously, this divine shell-fish has been held in a kind of superstitious reverence at the Manhattoes; as witness the temples erected to its cult in every street and lane and alley.

He was referring to the extensive number of oyster houses and taverns – more than 850 by 1874. Irving made friends with the British author Charles Dickens (1812–1870) during the first of two trips that Dickens made to the States, one in 1842 and another in 1868. Arriving in Boston for the 1842 visit, Dickens dined with Henry Wadsworth Longfellow and Cornelius Conway Felton, who would later become the president of Harvard. In a letter posted from New York later that trip, Dickens implored Felton, 'Come to England! Our oysters are small I know; they are said by Americans to be coppery, but our hearts are of the largest size.'

The Immigration Factor

A confluence of factors accounts for the expansion of oyster consumption in America in the 1800s: waterborne commerce, the establishment of a canning industry, the building of the transcontinental railroad between 1840 and 1860, the California Gold Rush of 1849, and unprecedented immigration of a European workforce streaming through Ellis Island. People and communities follow waterways and the blue lines on a map of the Mississippi, Ohio, Missouri and Illinois rivers, as well as the Erie Canal, could paint a map of oyster expansion. Boom towns such as Cincinnati, St Louis and New Orleans grew where riverboats could sail, bringing with them new industries, workers and the oysters to feed them. Oyster restaurants and taverns were opening all over America's larger waterfront cities. Boston's Union Oyster House is still the oldest restaurant in continuous service, and has been shucking and serving oysters since 1826. Two other restaurants still in service in the United States also originated because of oysters: New Orleans' Antoine's Restaurant, opened and made famous for their Oysters Rockefeller since 1840, and Tadich Grill in San Francisco, which has been serving dishes like the famous Hangtown Fry since 1849.

In 1819 New York City opened its first fish cannery, at first utilizing glass bottles for the packaging of oysters before switching to tin-plated cans in 1839. Until this time many consumers would shuck their own oysters or buy them from street vendors. The advent of canning created an entire new industry and the demand for a cheap workforce to propel its

The Hangtown Fry as presented at Tadich Grill, San Francisco, California, one of the oldest oyster-based restaurants in the United States.

enterprise, as well as the customer for their own product. Migrants were starting to head west and able to take with them the very cans of oysters they had grown accustomed to eating. A 9 January 1857 *New York Tribune* article describes a typical cannery: 'There are the openers [shuckers], the washers, the measurers, the fillers, the packers, etc., each of which performs only the duties pertaining to its own division.' At the Maggioni Canning Company in Port Royal, South Carolina, for example, children were engaged to shuck oysters for seven hours a day: four hours before school started and another three hours after school had finished – if they even went to school. Those that did not attend school worked fourteen-hour days, from 3 am until 5 pm, with a short break for lunch. The young boys would work as shuckers until they were old or strong enough to work on the boats. Young mothers would bring their children to work with them. Shucking and canning warehouses were frigid, as the bulk of the work was done during the coldest months. Averaging 65 quarts of oysters per day, at 2½ cents per quart, the children could earn upwards of $9 (about £2) per week. The leftover shells were burned in large kilns to make lime that was used in the building industry and crushed shells were used as poultry feed.

Most immigrant communities included oysters in their diet, even the Jews, who had previously forbidden their consumption. The large German-Jewish contingent, who predominantly came from Bavaria in the 1830s, settled in New York and blended with existing, already established Sephardic communities. The kosher laws of *treyf* were slackening as new gastronomic principles were being adopted. In 1869 Martin Smith's best-selling book *Sunshine and Shadow* described a meal 'containing oysters held at the home of an eminent

'All these children except babies shuck oysters and tend babies at the Pass Packing Co. I saw them all at work there long before daybreak. Photos taken at noon in the absence of the superintendent who refused me permission because of child labor agitation.' Pass Christian, Mississippi, *c*. 1912. Several of the boys on the far left are holding up their shucking knives.

Seven-year-old Rosie could not read or write and had already worked as an oyster shucker for over a year in 1913; from the Varn & Platt Canning Company in Bluffton, South Carolina.

Jewish businessman'; the reason such a forbidden food could be eaten, he explains, was that conformity to changing times and a new, adopted country was imperative: 'The oysters of Palestine were coppery and poisonous. Had the great lawgiver [Moses] enjoyed a fry or a stew of Saddlerocks or Chesapeake Bay oysters, he would have made an exception in their favor.' In the 1840s Croatian-Slovenian immigrants quickly headed south from Ellis Island towards the oyster-rich estuaries adjacent to the Mississippi River below New Orleans. The skills they had been honing for 2,000 years in the waters near Dubrovnik were easily transferred to the bayou and to this day Dalmatian Croatians are credited with developing the still-thriving Louisiana oyster industry. It was some of these very talented Croatians who made their way to San Francisco for the gold rush and opened the Tadich Grill.

Gold prospectors arriving in California in 1849 caused a population boom resulting in a considerable market pressure for oysters. Captain Charles J. W. Russell, originally from Virginia, is credited with introducing aquafarming to California by shipping fresh Olympias from Shoalwater Bay in Washington, up the Pacific coast. These oysters account for 90 per cent of the fresh oysters in California from 1850 to 1869, but by the 1880s the Shoalwater oysters were in decline due to over-harvesting. The completion of the transcontinental railroad meant that a consumer was not limited to locally grown oysters or those that were shipped from the Shoalwater trade. A newspaper advertisement in the *Alta California* on 22 October 1869 gloated about the first shipment of oysters to arrive from the other side of the country by train: 'The first carload of Baltimore and New York oysters in shells, cans, kegs, all in splendid order, has arrived, packed and shipped by the pioneer oyster house of the west, A. Booth, Chicago, Ill.' Within a short time, these eastern imports were outselling the Washington offerings. Seeing a preference for the Atlantic oyster and the success of locomotive transportation, the California farmers began experimenting and succeeding with eastern seed oysters in the San Francisco Bay. Sadly, this genus never thrived anywhere else on the West Coast, although attempts were made in Washington, Oregon and other California bays such as Humboldt and Tomales. Eventually, the San Francisco Bay oysters would suffer the same demise as their

Oysters! Oysters!

CAPT. RUSSELL, the pioneer of the Shoalwater Bay trade, and the particular pioneer in the Oyster Trade, has just received two more cargoes of these bivalves, for the satisfaction of our citizens, and to please their increasing taste for the good things of—the waters.

The last two cargoes consist of some 5,000 baskets of the best oysters yet brought to market, and we learn that Captain R. is planting them on the Oakland side of the bay. A friend at our elbow asks us, (as we tell of *planting oysters,*) if they will grow? We assure our friend that nothing increases faster by planting than OYSTERS.

Some may think but little of the announcement of the oyster trade on this coast, but it is an *important fact. Thousands and tens of tnousands of dollars* are thus retained in California, giving employment to vessels and men, that otherwise would go to the East for preserved oysters. Now we have them fresh and save the gold in the State.

East Coast counterparts and fall prey to sewage contamination and overfishing, but from 1888 to 1904, averaging more than $500,000 annually, oysters as a commodity for the state were exceeded in value only by whalebone as the most valuable fishery product.

In both Europe and the United States, there were many oyster-only taverns to attract gentlemen who liked to debate politics, as depicted in Richard Caton Woodville's *Politics in an Oyster House* of 1848. No one is sure how many oyster street vendors there were in either New York or London, but most heavily populated street corners would feature an oyster vendor that people could visit for a quick snack. John R. Philpots penned an exhaustive, two-volume tome titled *Oysters, And All About Them* in 1891, in which he speculates, 'It was estimated in 1864 that seven hundred millions of oysters were consumed annually in London, and considerably more than that number in the provinces.'

What was happening ecologically was harrowing: the diminishment of the wild oyster and the depletion of natural oyster beds. Beginning in 1825, oysters from the Chesapeake had to be transplanted to Narragansett Bay, Delaware Bay, Raritan Bay and Long Island Sound; thus the age of the schooner, the skipjack and scientific cultivation techniques began. By the 1870s more than two million bushels a year of Chesapeake seed were being moved to other estuaries, a practice that continued for another thirty years. In the southern hemisphere, local traders had been shipping oysters to New Zealand from Sydney and Melbourne since 1845, but fisheries there were being destroyed by overfishing as well. October 1866 saw the passing of the New Zealand Oyster Fisheries Act in an attempt to protect the diminishing oyster beds. In Australia, oyster farmers were starting to grow oysters on available organic material such as sticks and other shells. By 1888 Australian oyster beds were also depleted to such an extent that the importation of rock oyster spat from New Zealand was required. The Zeeland region of the Netherlands had pulled three million oysters from their beds in 1861, but three years later, only 50,000 were sold. By the 1880s the U.S. oyster industry employed almost 53,000 persons, harvesting over 700 million oysters a year. Between 1880 and 1910, oyster production was at a peak in the United States, with harvests producing 72.5 million kg (160 million lb) of oyster meat per year – more than the entire rest of the world.

This increase in demand created an explosion that resulted in what are now known as 'The Oyster Wars'. Legislation had been passed in 1830 in Maryland which restricted the harvesting of oysters to residents only. Maryland had outlawed the fishing practice of dredging (the mass scraping of the ocean floor with nets) and required the issuing of permits for oyster harvesting. Virginia, however, continued to allow dredging until 1879. As the Chesapeake's supply was diminishing, many armed and organized dredgers violated the laws as seasoned fisherman became modern-day pirates. Illegal oystering resulted in many skirmishes and violent conflicts that were fought up to 1959, when the fisheries police were finally disbanded after the killing of a Virginia waterman who was dredging illegally.

In New York City alone from 1860 to 1900, the population increased ninefold from over 800,000 to almost 3.5 million. By 1940 the population was almost 7.5 million. Following the Civil War (1861–5), the United States became an industrial giant and a leader on the world stage. Worldwide industries were reinventing themselves as there was now petroleum refining, electrical power and steel manufacturing. In the mid-1800s most Americans earned their living on farms, but within fifty years the American economy came to rely on factories and the workers to keep these factories running. The increase in population meant that oysters became a cheap and easy food source and for a while they were a readily accessible commodity. The struggling worker could rely on the 'Canal Street Plan' that offered unlimited oysters on the half-shell for 6 cents at oyster taverns throughout New York City. The Fulton Street Market was selling 50,000 oysters a day in 1887. The British were eating 1.5 billion oysters a year, many shipped from America. This industrial revolution, which brought people from the countryside into crowded cities, ostensibly turned a blind eye to slave labour practices.

By 1900 oyster farmers in the Gulf of Mexico and the Carolinas were sending headhunters to Baltimore specifically to seek out newly arrived Polish immigrants because they

Richard Caton Woodville, *Politics in an Oyster House*, 1848.

were known to be pliable, hard-working and affordable. Advertisements beckoned workers to the lush, warm tropics and promised wages of 15 cents an hour for men and 12½ cents for women. Sadly, whole families would relocate only to discover that just one job was available and the pay was a fraction of what was advertised. The rest of the family would be offered shucking jobs at 5 cents for an agreed-upon measure. According to one worker, a measure 'should be four and one-half pounds but is usually more than seven to eight pounds'. It was essentially slavery and Polish foremen were hired to manage the workers, since many had not yet learned English. Stories exist of these foremen coercing the workers' wives into sexual service in exchange for better working conditions for their husbands and families. The work was back-breaking and demoralizing and the workers suffered the consequences of unrelentingly poor conditions. Despite the horrific conditions, it was African Americans who would become an underlying power within the oyster industry. Known as Black Jacks, when the Emancipation Proclamation was executed in 1863, these black workers could succeed where others struggled or even failed. In a step up from the indentured servitude they had been subjected to by slave owners, a modest outlay in equipment enabled able-bodied workers to make a very respectable living. Some figures suggest that within a decade of the end of the Civil War, over 70,000 freed black slaves were working in oyster beds all along the East Coast. In South Carolina alone, for example, the oyster industry was the most valuable fishery from the late 1880s to just after the Second World War. In 1902 oyster production accounted for 45 per cent of all the fisheries reporting to the state commissioner. It was important in providing steady work for African American harvesters and shuckers when no other employment existed, and the industry sustained that ethnicity from about 1900, through the Great Depression and into the Second World War.

6

The Gilded Age

Starting roughly around 1870, the 'Gilded Age' (as coined by Mark Twain) commenced. Also known as the belle époque, it was a period in history characterized by peace, prosperity and excess, just before the horrors of the First World War of 1914–18. Wealthy citizens' demand for oysters elevated what was once a simple man's dinner to one of elegance and refinement. With almost two million immigrants arriving in America in 1850 alone, there was a marked dichotomy between the wealth and opulence of the nouveaux riches and the poverty and destitution of the incoming immigrants who provided the huge, inexpensive workforce, who had been raised on oysters and wished to continue eating them. Unfortunately, all these people crowded the cities where infrastructure and lack of proper sanitation would cause epidemics and pandemics, almost killing the oyster industry and certainly killing many of its consumers.

On 10 May 1869 in Promontory Summit in Utah, a golden spike was driven to connect the two massive labours of the Central Pacific and the Union Pacific railroad lines, creating the Transcontinental Railroad. This act linked together an entire continent with railroad stops. With the railroads came dining cars, train station hostelries, Harvey Girls and oysters. The system of harvesting, packaging and shipping via railcars was known as the 'oyster express' and many dining establishments would advertise which scheduled train swould be carrying oysters so that customers could plan their meals accordingly. By 1890, 225-kg (500-lb) barrels of oysters shipped to Chicago cost $7.50. Some government figures indicate that less than one gallon in 2,000 was lost or damaged. Books like *The Steward's Handbook* (1889) by Jessup Whitehead instructed in the service of these new types of travellers. As many headed west to find their fortune in mining and farming, others had already found their fortune and were looking to expand their wealth. Despite the frontier locations, many proprietors attempted to provide the fineries their customers demanded, were accustomed to or aspired towards. Louis 'French Louie' du Puy (1844–1900) was one of these immigrants who had chased the American dream. After failed attempts as a reporter and a miner, and a stint in the Army, he purchased a small, dilapidated bakery and turned it into one of the foremost elegant hotels in the Midwest, the famous Hotel de Paris in Georgetown, Colorado. Opened in 1875, the hotel boasted Limoges china, elegant flatware and imported linens and in 1893 was one of the first establishments to be wired for electric lighting. Being 3,200 km (2,000 mi.) from a major city was no impediment to French Louie's ability to provide delicacies such as imported anchovies in olive oil, turtle soup, porterhouse steaks with truffles and a full offering of oysters: on the half shell for 65 cents a dozen, stewed for 75 cents a dozen or fried for 80 cents a dozen.

The Gourmet's Guide to Europe (the Michelin guide of its day), written by Algernon Bastard in 1903, offered oyster and restaurant suggestions for the traveller. Brittany was considered the land of butter and eggs, but Bastard made special note to head towards the coast: 'Cancale of course has its oyster-beds, and the esculent bivalve can be eaten within sight of the mud-flat on which it erstwhile reposed.' Or in Paris, 'You will find a great variety of oysters . . . at Prunier's, in the Rue Duphot, and the dishes of the house – soup, sole, steak – are all cooked with oysters as a foundation, sauce, or garnish.' In Paris specifically, *séparées* ('separate rooms') were thriving, small and very intimate dining establishments catering to the devotees of night-time debauchery with breakfast offerings of oysters and champagne. This was also an era when wealthy American families like the Vanderbilts and Whitneys married off their daughters to landed gentry and royalty in England. While the poor were consuming their oysters with brown bread and beer, the elite were relishing their oysters with caviar and champagne at restaurants like Delmonico's in New York, Harvey's in Washington, DC – where every president from Ulysses S. Grant to Franklin D. Roosevelt dined before it closed in 1932 – and Antoine's in New Orleans. During this era restaurant service changed from a classic style of presentation, *service à la française*, where every course for an entire meal was served at once (now known as family style), to *service à la russe* (served in the Russian style), in which each individual course is served sequentially with its own specialized plate, utensil and beverage pairing. These grand offerings were traditionally eight or ten courses – or more – and always started with oysters (or caviar) accompanied by champagne. The meal would then continue with a soup or consommé, paired with Madeira or sherry, seguing to a fish with a white wine, a roast with red wine and so on, finishing with a vintage port and tea or coffee with cheeses.

The celebrity chefs of the day included Charles Ranhofer (1836–1899) of Delmonico's in New York and the Savoy's Auguste Escoffier (1846–1935) in London. Escoffier was quite emphatic about the illustrious bivalve as he states in his cookbook *Le Guide culinaire* (1903): 'Though oysters are best raw, there are so many culinary preparations of which they form the leading ingredient, and such a number of garnishing uses to which they may be put, that I feel compelled to mention some of these.' Just a few of the recipes that Escoffier lists include *Huîtres à la favorite*, *Huîtres au gratin*, *Huîtres à la Mornay* and several more. Ranhofer's magnum opus, *The Epicurean* (1894), has no fewer than thirty oyster recipes, including Philadelphia style, Viennese, stuffed and fried, and Indian style with curry. For these multi-hour meals, which started with raw oysters, specially designed oyster plates were used so that the diner would not have to soil their hands with rough and potentially dirty oyster shells. It was far neater and cleaner to serve the shucked oyster – including its liquor – on an elegant plate with a sterling fork that would help transport the delicate morsel to the anxiously awaiting mouth. This fork, stylized to mimic Neptune's trident, was three-tined and relatively small: a proper size in relation to the oyster it would be spearing. The utensil could be elaborate or plain, but an oyster would never be served without an appropriate utensil. If stewed, there was even a special spoon to serve the oyster reminiscent of its very self. The oyster plate – simple or elegant, garish or kitschy – came in three basic styles:

> The Geometric, where a perfect circle of six oyster moulds is evenly laid out with a space in the middle for sauce.

> The Turkey, which has only five moulds, versus six for the Geometric.

> The Kidney – or Crescent-shaped – most often produced by Union Porcelain Works.

Today, collectible oyster plates can cost from as little as £8 ($10) to ten times that amount for rare, hand-painted versions. Some may come with floral designs or sea creatures draped over the plate. Often the oyster crevice will be uneven – mimicking the undulating inner shape of the oyster itself – with the ubiquitous dark smudge delineating where the adductor muscle had attached itself to the shell. They were so popular in their era that Rutherford B. Hayes (1822–1893), the nineteenth president of the United States, had a set of oyster plates commissioned for the White House. Designed by Theodore R. Davis (1840–1894), an artist who worked for *Harper's Weekly*, the plates were made by the Haviland Company of Limoges, France, and were the genesis of what is now known as a Turkey Plate. The set was designed to feature an

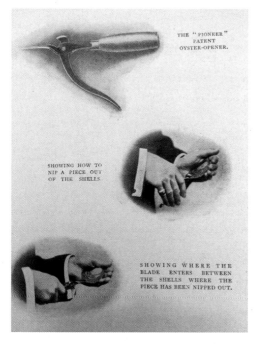

THE "PIONEER" PATENT OYSTER-OPENER.

SHOWING HOW TO NIP A PIECE OUT OF THE SHELLS

SHOWING WHERE THE BLADE ENTERS BETWEEN THE SHELLS WHERE THE PIECE HAS BEEN NIPPED OUT.

During the Victorian era, many new gadgets were invented to make oyster dining easier for all, from waiters to the home enthusiast. This was just one such gadget.

The Victorians were masters of design, creating the most elegant offerings of oyster utensils, from the large oyster serving spoon to the smaller, intricate oyster forks.

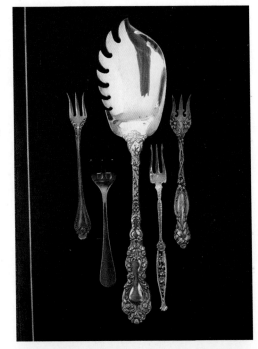

This, the only oyster plate ever made for the White House, was produced under the presidency of Rutherford B. Hayes in 1877.

open Blue Point oyster and a closed Raccoon oyster (now extinct); the cluster of the two mimicked the outline of America's native bird, the turkey.

Oysters Rockefeller, the most illustrious of all oyster recipes, would not have been served on one of these special dishes. The porcelain or clay used to make these plates would not have survived the grilling (broiling) process required for its preparation. Oysters Rockefeller comes with many legends, stories and different recipes. One such recipe was developed by Jules Alciatore (1862–1928), son of the famous Antoine Alciatore (d. 1875), who opened Antoine's in New Orleans in 1840. As a chef, Jules trained in some of the great kitchens in France before returning to America. It is said that he adapted an escargot recipe when snails were in short supply, creating a sauce (some claim it is a béchamel and others insist it includes cheese) with some spices, wilted greens and breadcrumbs to top a freshly opened oyster that is then grilled. The exact recipe that is still prepared at Antoine's is a closely guarded secret. Roy F. Guste Jr, Jules' great-great grandson, confirms that 'the sauce is basically a purée of a number of green vegetables other than spinach.' Antoine's claims that the dish was named for John D. Rockefeller, at that time the richest man in the world. Another legend has it that the dish was introduced to New York – after its invention in New Orleans – by Chef Ranhofer at Delmonico's with Diamond Jim Brady (1856–1917) as the inspiration for the dish. Brady, a financier and philanthropist who was known to frequent Delmonico's for its Oysters Rockefeller, transformed the dish into a symbol of the elite as the green of the spinach was emblematic of the colour green in paper money. Diamond Jim was known to consume an entire bushel of oysters (around 100 oysters) in a single sitting, adding to the mystique of the well-to-do and their reputation for over-consumption.

The middle and lower classes dined more humbly, creating simpler dishes like stews with their oysters at home. Besides raw and on the half shell, the bivalves were offered up as Sunday dinner: grilled, stewed, pan-roasted or in an omelette or a pie. In middle-class dining halls, oyster feasts were offered up as entertainment as well by a showman – usually an Irishman – known as The Patty Man. In eight nimble and awe-inspiring steps he would deftly fill pre-cooked puff pastry shells with oysters and gravy before the eyes of eager diners. An article in the *Eugene Register* on 5 April 1884, by an unnamed reporter, described:

> Often my appetite would have inclined me toward the 10-cent sandwich but I passed by this economic food and had gone to that particular part of the restaurant sacred to the patty. Usually it is thronged. Long successions of oyster-patty eaters wait patiently here for their delectable morsels. To the extreme left of the counter stands the oyster patty man, and to the right his rival, the chicken patty man. But for one chicken patty eaten there are fifty oyster patties devoured.

Death and Disease

In both Europe and America, the combination of over-population, poor sanitation and the oyster's unique breeding environment created a perfect storm in the dissemination of diseases – specifically cholera and typhoid fever. Both cholera and typhoid are deadly bacterial diseases that are transmitted mainly through drinking water and food that have been contaminated with faecal matter. In cities, oyster vendors were busy selling their products on streets shared with butchers and other fish vendors who openly eviscerated their wares and discarded the carcasses and unwanted bits into the gutters. Tenement blocks had few public facilities for washing and many tenants would dispose of their refuse into these same gutters. All of this sewage drained into the nearby waterways, which were the main source of drinking water and also led directly to the oyster beds. Cholera's first appearance as a pandemic was in India in 1817, travelling throughout Asia and the Middle East in the 1820s. Russia and Eastern Europe saw it next, by 1830, and then it arrived in London and Paris in 1832, killing 13,000 Parisians alone. Three different cholera pandemics occurred in the 1800s in Kent in England, a maritime county. When it crossed the Atlantic in June of 1832, close to half of New York City's population – more than 100,000 people – fled the city in fear. No one knew how it spread and it seemed unstoppable. Death from cholera is swift, often within a few days, and mortality rates were a staggering 90 per

Oysters Rockefeller.

cent. The 1854 New York cholera epidemic became known as 'the oyster panic' in the press; it was more noted among the gentry than the poor, in part because the illiteracy rates meant that newspapers were not read by the poorer victims of the blight.

Typhoid fever was more preventable and less likely to be fatal than cholera, but equally contributory to the oyster's demise. Sir William Broadbent (1835–1907), reporting in the *British Medical Journal*, accounted for several dozen cases all over Europe: two fatalities in Berlin, 'a number of cases' traced to Italy and France, and 181 cases in Brighton alone from 1893 to 1896 (where nearly one-third were attributed to eating raw shellfish). At Connecticut's Wesleyan University in October of 1893, 26 cases were found in three different fraternities where the only common denominator was a nearby oyster purveyor. Another large outbreak led to the complete demise of the Emsworth oyster beds near Hampshire in England when 63 people became ill and four died after eating oysters at a 1902 mayoral banquet in Winchester. Even our astute Mr Bastard, in his *Gourmet's Guide to Europe*, offered warnings to the savvy traveller: 'A man who eats oysters in Russia, eats his own damnation, and at a high price in both senses; they are both costly and poisonous in a town where typhoid is easily contracted.'

While water contamination was shown to explain the typhoid outbreaks, one way for the virus to be transmitted was through carriers like Mary Mallon (1869–1938) – the infamous Typhoid Mary – who worked as a cook for several families in Oyster Bay, including Charles Henry Warren, a wealthy New York banker. It is suspected that she personally infected more than fifty people, three of whom perished. An even more dangerous way to become infected was a process in the shellfish industry of 'fattening' or 'plumping', whereby the oystermen would harvest the oysters from the estuary, but store them in baskets just below the water line near sewage outtakes. Transferring the oysters from dense to less dense water several days before going to market gave the oysters the appearance of being bigger than they actually were. A manual published in 1920 titled 'Standard Methods for the Bacteriological Examination of Shellfish' gave insight into the public health issue, but it was mostly ignored until the deadliest occurrence of oyster-borne typhoid occurred in the winter of 1924–5. Simultaneous reports from New York, Washington, DC, and Chicago had people suffering: more than 1,500 were sick and 150 dead. It was eventually traced back to a West Sayville, New York, distribution company that had been 'floating its oysters'. Considerable health and safety laws went into effect because of this tragedy, but not before oyster demand plummeted by 50 to 80 per cent worldwide.

There is a dichotomy between the fear of oysters due to the associated diseases caused or carried by the shellfish and the health benefits which many doctors ascribed to them – especially at the end of the twentieth century. The Victorians were known for many bizarre health fads, including the use of arsenic soap, Fletcherism (extensive chewing of one's food) and the popularity of sanitariums, where guests could avail themselves of enemas of all kinds, thermal and sulphuric baths and electric shock therapy. It should come as no surprise that the oyster had its health proponents, as doctors from every era have promoted its benefits for a healthy diet, but the apex of this concept came from the Edwardians, who devoted innumerable magazine articles and books to the subject. One of the beautifully bound books on the subject at the turn of the century was *The Mollusc Paramount, Being a Comprehensive Treatise on the Oyster in Relation to the Epicure, the Invalid, the Physician & the Plain Citizen* (1909), which delves into great depth on the health benefits of oysters. Numerous doctors expanded upon the oyster's curative benefits, including Dr Pasquier, who 'advised their use for persons of intemperate habits, who, in consequence of excess, suffer from exhaustion and depression . . . and in some cases they have succeeded where all other "remedies" have failed'. It was well known that oysters were good for 'female ailments':

ANCIENT NATIVES OF BRITAIN, ENCAMPED NEAR COLCHESTER.
(From a curious Glyptic in possession of the Author.)

Illustration from F.H.E. Pankow, *The Mollusc Paramount* (1909).

at no time are they more valuable than at that period of a woman's married life when nausea is prevalent. At such time a few fresh oysters taken raw in their own liquor, with no addition other than a little pepper, will prove a most effective remedy.

A Victorian-era precursor to the oyster shooter of the twenty-first century was a 'tea' for the infirm that was concocted from oysters, beef broth and arrowroot. It was believed to cure anything from depression to pulmonary complaints, if administered under medical supervision.

J. Harvey Kellogg (1852–1943), famous for building the Battle Creek Sanitarium in Michigan and an early advocate of vegetarianism, is mostly known today for inventing the cornflake. He did not have a very high opinion of oysters (or any meats, for that matter). During a speech given to the Michigan State Horticultural Society in 1907 he declared:

> The first thing on the bill of fare was oysters. I did not want any. Why? In the first place, the oyster is a scavenger; his business is to lick off the slime at the bottom of the sea; you catch the oyster down there; he has got his broad lips open and licking off the slime; he likes that slime because it is full of germs . . . Lemon juice will kill not only oyster germs, but typhoid fever germs. Oyster germs are typhoid fever germs. That is why people get typhoid fever sometimes by eating raw oysters. If you are fond of typhoid fever germs, oysters on the half shell will be a good way to get them.

Obviously Kellogg was spot on with the oyster/typhoid affiliation, but incorrect on his scientific analysis. He is also wrong about the lemon juice. Dare I say, deadly wrong? It was erroneously believed by many doctors that the acid in lemon juice would destroy typhoid bacilli. Newspaper announcements proclaimed the astonishingly false claims that 'In addition to the use of lemon juice in drinking water the [Chicago Health] department recommends that the juice be freely sprinkled on oysters when eaten raw.' Since old habits die hard, quartered lemons have been served with oysters ever since and are now considered a traditional garnish. Medical journals at the time tried to dissuade the misinformation, but their warnings regrettably fell on deaf ears:

> The laity will continue to rest secure from typhoid fever so long as lemons are obtainable, and the injury done by the careless propagation of this fallacious teaching is incalculable, since the newspaper medical writer finds it less interesting to his readers to correct an error than to foster one.

We can thank the love of oysters for a surprising development in take-home or takeaway dining. Around 1894, when a working-class stiff wanted to bring oysters home for his wife to cook, he wouldn't have wanted the additional labour of having to shuck the oysters himself. Also, as there is considerable skill needed in the shucking process, it was common for the oyster seller to do the work and offer the shucked meat in a small, paper oyster pail. As the oyster beds were becoming over-farmed and the local oyster vendor was soon out of a job, the manufacturers of the oyster pail found themselves with a surplus which – after the Second World War – were relegated to the sales of takeaway Chinese food. What is now recognizable as a Chinese food container originated with the oyster industry.

There is some debate about when the Gilded Age ended; it was either with the death of Queen Victoria in 1901 or the

The Walrus and Carpenter happen upon some unwitting – and shoe-wearing – oysters who are ultimately consumed by the two characters, in John Tenniel's illustration from Lewis Carroll's *Through the Looking-glass and What Alice Found There* (1871).

start of the First World War in 1914. For oystermen in America, it was the Panic of 1893, as America's rise as a world power practically disintegrated owing to one of the worst depressions in the country's history. Several decades of over-speculation in the stock market and new businesses, rapid industrial growth, the influx of immigrants and the profiteering of corrupt businessmen resulted in the ruin of the United States economy. More than 16,000 businesses closed, sending three million people into unemployment and causing substantial labour strikes. Almost 650 banks collapsed. What happened between the last decade of the nineteenth century and the first decade of the twentieth century would change just about everything for oyster lovers, oyster chefs and oyster fishermen.

7
The Twentieth-century Oyster

The beginning of the twentieth century is earmarked with change, tragedy and, ultimately, triumph. Oyster beds were quickly becoming overfished and that fact was beginning to be noticed and addressed. The depletion of the oyster beds and other fishes helped create the Royal Commission on Sea Fisheries in England, headed by T. H. Huxley, the noted biologist and Darwin proponent. In America, the Oyster Growers and Dealers Association (OGDA) banded together with the National Association of Shellfish Commissioners (NASC) in 1909 to deal with the demise of their industry. At that time, thirteen American states produced 88 per cent of the world's oyster production. In 1915 the two groups reorganized to become the National Association of Fisheries Commissioners (NAFC) and by 1930 it was known as the National Shellfisheries Association (NSA), which is still in operation to this day and includes all members of the industry.

With the world entering a new century, oyster beds all over the East Coast of the United States and in the UK were closing, some owing to depletion of product and others because pollution had made their product unsaleable. The industrialization of the food industry by producers of dairy products, meat, sweets and more were all affected by sanitation

The culling and sorting of oysters in Whitstable was back-breaking work.

issues that plagued the growth of the oyster industry. Food science was a new study and studies of 'germ theory' in connection with food consumption went from folklore to fact in the span of ten years. Investigators were able to pinpoint a relationship between sewage disposal and illnesses. The 'Pure Food Law' was established in 1906 by the United States Congress, the same day that President Theodore Roosevelt signed the Federal Meat Inspection Act. These laws brought about more stringent regulations in the handling, packing and shipping of oysters. These steps helped clean up a dirty and deadly food production industry, but many consumers were still being cautious. The UK suffered a handful of additional typhoid outbreaks in the first decade of the century and several of those afflicted filed lawsuits – the oyster consumers sued restaurants and the victims won compensation. It has been speculated by scientists that just before America's colonial war of the nineteenth century, there were three trillion oysters in New York City's waters alone. By 1927 the last of the New York oyster fisheries had shut down as the connection between typhoid and oysters was verified. The oysters that were being served in that city had to be imported from New England.

As prophesied in *The Oyster* (1891) by William Kenneth Brooks, 'The demand for Chesapeake oysters has outgrown the natural supply. The remedy . . . is to increase the supply by artificial means.' Many were beginning to listen and in

By the turn of the last century, the canning of oysters had become a huge industry.

1902 Japan began sending seed to Puget Sound to help their depleting beds. There were successes in both America and Europe until the First World War started and the world's attention was directed elsewhere. There were no more fancy dinner parties or overt displays of excess wealth. It was now a world of frugality and reserve. Rationing became the norm during the war. The people's love of oysters had not waned but when the war ended, at least in America, they were much harder to come by. The saloons and drinking establishments where oysters had been so popular when Charles Dickens visited were closed from 1918 to 1930 owing to Prohibition.

In Europe, literati expatriates such as Sylvia Beach and James Joyce were hobnobbing in Paris with Gertrude Stein and Alice B. Toklas (who provides an Oysters Rockefeller in the recipe section of their famous cookbook). In 1921 Ernest Hemingway arrived in Paris with designs of making a name for himself as a reporter. One can just imagine him sitting in a café while penning his posthumously published *A Moveable Feast*:

> As I ate the oysters with their strong taste of the sea and their faint metallic taste that the cold white wine washed away, leaving only the sea taste and the succulent texture, and as I drank their cold liquid from each shell and washed it down with the crisp taste of the wine, I lost the empty feeling and began to be happy and to make plans.

We know that Hemingway 'closed up the story in the notebook and put it [in his] inside pocket and asked the waiter for a dozen "portugueses" and a half-carafe of dry white wine'. Sadly, in 1969 the Portuguese oyster (*Crassostrea angulata*) succumbed to one of the many genetic diseases that have

afflicted oysters, and is no longer commercially farmed anywhere in the world.

While Hemingway was waxing poetic about oysters, the
American composer and songwriter Cole Porter (1891–1964)
crafted a hysterical satire on the nouveaux riches' attempts to
climb the social ladder in the guise of an oyster.

> Down by the sea lived a lonesome oyster,
> Ev'ry day getting sadder and moister.
> He found his home life awf'lly wet,
> And longed to travel with the upper set.

The song relates the tale of an oyster who has been scooped
up by a chef, prepared and served to the wife of a million-
aire who, after lunch, goes yachting and gets seasick, thereby
vomiting the oyster back into the ocean. The oyster offers the
commentary upon his consumption and demise:

> Back once more where he started from,
> He murmured, 'I haven't a single qualm,
> For I've had a taste of society,
> And society has had a taste of me.'

Between the world wars, as the transplanted Japanese
seed was thriving on the West Coast, 2,000 adult oysters from
Samish Bay, Washington, and twenty cases of seed from
Japan were shipped to the Chesapeake in 1926 in an attempt
to rebuild the crumbling industry on the East Coast. By 1932
British Columbia had its first major spawning of Pacific
oysters. As the Depression descended on a weary nation,
according to Melbourne Romaine Carriker in her National
Shellfisheries Association history (2004), '[Oyster] production
fell 50 per cent and by 1933 perhaps 15 million were out of

work.' Franklin D. Roosevelt's New Deal, established between 1933 and 1938, began an economic upswing that would accelerate towards the Second World War, but the oyster as a family staple would never again see the explosion of availability or desirability on the scale it had experienced in the 1800s. The oyster became a speciality food, still desired and loved, but beef and chicken supplanted the oyster as a mainstay for most households.

The year 1939 brought the start of the Second World War in Europe and the transportation of seed from Japan to the United States was halted. The onslaught of both world wars saw a disruption of oyster production, but the advent of commercial aircraft after the Second World War helped revive a struggling oyster industry with the first air shipments of oysters by Flying Tigers, the first scheduled cargo airline in the United States, in 1952. The war severely damaged Japan's Miyagi and Hiroshima oyster beds and the British beds were also severely diminished, despite Great Britain having been the European powerhouse of oysters for centuries. In the 1950s in the UK, the Ministry of Agriculture, Fisheries and Food's Directorate of Fisheries Research began investigating various methods of encouraging natural settlement of oyster larvae – 'spat' – at a laboratory in Conwy on the north coast of Wales. The first attempts were made with transplanting seed from Portuguese oysters, but the Welsh waters were found to be too cold for that genus. The next attempts brought *Crassostrea gigas* (Pacific) seed into British waters. This again proved unsuccessful. According to the Ministry's documents, the

> failure to utilize existing seed stock is due to (i) lack of expertise in growing the small oysters [2 mm to 3 mm] to a size suitable for laying on oyster grounds, (ii) the large expenditure needed for trays, rafts and labour

in order to on-grow the small seed, (iii) the lack of an assured market outlet.

In the UK, they did what others all over the world were beginning to do: investigate and utilize fully controlled hatcheries.

The French oyster beds mostly escaped the ravages of the world wars and the country was in a better position to restart its oyster industry. In the 1950s a system known as 'rack and bag' cultivation, which was similar to what Orata had established in ancient Rome, was utilized. With the addition of racks, the bags of oysters are occasionally turned to prevent the oysters from growing onto the bag itself or another oyster, which allows for even growing conditions. The steel racks are situated into the sand or onto silt and since the oysters are kept from lying on the bottom, they feed better and grow faster. This method also protects the oysters from predators. This simple development in oyster culturing is considered by some to be an improvement over the traditional beach method, where the oysters are placed in shallow waters. *Affinage* (refinement) is an additional process and would be the last step utilized by growers to 'finish' an oyster. Since the oyster has gained character from its environment, it is possible for a grower to manipulate their final product by changing its living conditions. The best visible example of *affinage* can be seen in the famous Marennes-Oléron oysters, which are green in colour. The story goes that Louis XIV of France ordered oysters from Marennes-Oléron for his new wife, Madame de Maintenon, who, as she had not expected to see green oysters, suspected the kitchen staff of attempting regicide and ordered the oysters be discarded. The king was bereft and explained that the oysters of Marennes-Oléron were supposed to be green and that they were considered a delicacy. What happens is that the oysters feed on a microalgae known as *Navicula ostrea*, although the French have dubbed it *Navicule bleue* (blue navicula). Creating green oysters is an extreme example of what many oyster farmers do to manipulate and 'create' artisanal oysters.

One of the side-effects of the Second World War was the world's reliance on pre-packaged meals. While their men were on the battlefields, women had entered the workforce in unprecedented numbers as widespread male enlistment left gaping holes in the industrial labour force. This necessitated easing the burdens of home life with frozen TV dinners and other canned food products. In 1954 Campbell's made advancements in soup-making with the introduction of frozen soups. Fast flash-freezing processes made for a high-quality product with varieties that included snapper, clam chowder, green pea with ham, cream of potato and cream of shrimp. The oyster stew was a favourite and was only discontinued in frozen form in 1972 when technological advances made it

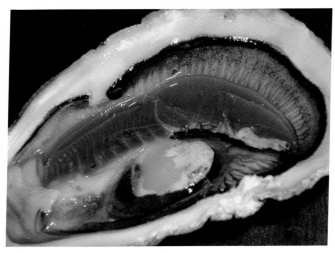

The oysters of Marennes-Oléron are often green, from the micro-algae *Navicula ostrea*.

Is the luxury of its flavor worth the extra cost?

*(She'll know...
and so will you the
moment you taste it)*

People who know fine food will wonder why this costs so little.

Green Pea with Ham
Oyster Stew • Clam Chowder
Old-Fashioned Vegetable with Beef
Cream of Shrimp • Cream of Potato

Here's oyster stew for folks with definite feelings on the subject. It's made with ocean-fresh oysters . . . simmered with all their good juices in fresh milk and special seasonings . . . and enough butter to float in golden pools on top. Then Campbell's freezes it fast—to hold all that wonderful flavor.

Discriminating people won't be surprised that this elegant oyster stew is higher priced. The wonder is that it costs so *little*. (As little as 13 cents per serving.)

Why don't you treat your family to Frozen Oyster Stew soon? Pick up a can or two next time you pass your grocer's freezer.

OYSTER STEW

FROZEN *by Campbell's*

Campbell's soup created a frozen oyster stew that was a favourite of customers for over five decades.

impossible for Campbell's to utilize the same ingredients in their regular, condensed soup creations. There was an outcry from consumers but, alas, frozen soups were no more. Many consoled themselves with the condensed oyster stew that Campbell's offered until sometime in 2011, when the product was discontinued entirely due to pollution levels affecting shellfish-growing areas in Korea, where Campbell's had sourced their oysters.

The end of the twentieth century saw a demise in the oyster industry due to overharvesting and the spread of diseases. This time, instead of human diseases such as typhoid and cholera, it would be oyster diseases that would inflict and decimate large portions of the American industry. In the 1950s and '60s two deadly parasites appeared on the East Coast of the United States and in the Gulf of Mexico: MSX (caused by the *Haplosporidium nelsoni* parasite) and Dermo (*Perkinsus marinus*). While neither makes oysters unsafe for human consumption, in some locations like the Delaware Bay as many as 90 to 95 per cent of the oysters died. An entirely different disease, now known as Denman Island disease, appeared in British Columbia and killed 30 per cent of the oysters there during its initial outbreak. The MSX and Dermo diseases did not affect the West Coast of the United States and Canada. With the benefit of additional disease-resistant Japanese seed, the oyster business on the West Coast was helped to grow until the 1970s, when the Japanese seed was no longer required.

Worldwide, the knowledge of science and diseases has been a driving force in helping the oyster regain its foothold as a consumable. An upsurge in the industry began in the 1970s with plantings and new beds being seeded all over the world. Tasmania became a powerhouse of breeding stock, providing spat that made the commercial farming of Australian oyster species the fourth-largest worldwide aquaculture industry. In 1980, after an accidental introduction of *Crassostrea gigas* in Argentina, the formation of a natural bank near Buenos Aires encouraged additional cultivation and today the seed continues to be extracted from that very bank. In Morocco, the Oualidia lagoon just south of Casablanca was established in the mid-1980s and is now known as a pre-eminent location for quality oysters. India was another country that took huge strides forward in oyster production, as the Central Marine Fisheries Research Institute initiated a pearl culture programme in 1972. This enabled an expansion of their technological resources required for the development of new strains of edible oysters. Most notable is an Indian backwater oyster (*Crassostrea bilineata*) abundant in the coastal waters of Tamil Nadu.

For sheer growth and expansion of oyster farming as an industry, China leads the way with more than ten institutes involved in mariculture research, most of which are driven towards improving oyster culture. China's production numbers are dizzying for just the *Crassostrea gigas* (Pacific) oyster alone: of the more than 4.38 million tonnes grown globally, 84 per cent is produced in China. Japan and South Korea each produce in excess of 200,000 tonnes and France, a distant fourth, 115,000 tonnes. Of the 46 oyster-producing countries worldwide, the only other countries able to provide the bivalve to eager consumers on a grand scale are the United States (with 43,000 tonnes) and Taiwan (with 23,000 tonnes).

With all this oyster love, it is not surprising that celebrations to honour the bivalve exist on every continent. Taking a cue from the fourteenth-century St Denys Fair in Colchester, oyster festivals have been established the world over. In Brazil, their National Oyster and Azorean Culture Festival is known as Fenaostra and is held in Florianópolis, Santa Catarina, where over 90 per cent of Brazil's oysters are farmed. Fenaostra is one of the few festivals that crowns a local queen and her court. The Pick-n-Pay Knysna Oyster Festival in South Africa started in 1983 and is held in July. The Miyajima Oyster Festival in Hiroshima was the first food festival to gain national acclaim in Japan after the Second World War. In America, 5 August

Guinness stout and oysters has been a favourite pairing for generations.

is National Oyster Day and many festivals are held around the country. The 1959 festival started in Galway, Ireland, is considered one of more internationally recognized Irish festivals after St Patrick's Day. Drawing more than 22,000 visitors, Galway's oyster festival includes a classic shucking competition with the likes of Toronto-based Patrick McMurray, the world record holder for shucking 38 oysters in one minute. Its grand allure is undoubtedly the combination of oysters and stout. The 'tradition' of pairing oysters with stout beer cannot be historically pinpointed, although Guinness stout has been advertising their affinity for decades. The British prime minister Benjamin Disraeli (1804–1881), in an 1837 letter to his sister, cited a rather happy repast: 'I dined, or rather supped, at the Carlton with a large party of the flower of our side, off oysters, Guinness and broiled bones, and got to bed at half-past twelve. Thus ended the most remarkable day hitherto of my life.' It is easy to hearken back a hundred years and envision a tired dockworker stumbling into a Galway pub after a hard day harvesting oysters. Hunkering down to the bar, he needs sustenance in the form of a pint of stout and shucked oysters. Consumed with hearty Irish brown bread and butter, it is a very comforting and easy pairing; a workaday alternative to the white wine pairing.

One is likely to inquire of oyster stout, a heavy, thick black beer made with oysters, which has a number of folkloric points of origination. One attribution references the first creation of an oyster stout in 1929 in New Zealand, although no one seems to know which brewery first started the practice, citing that an oyster extract produced in New Zealand during the late 1920s was used in brewing to improve head retention. Ezra Johnson-Greenough, via his well-researched blog, NewSchoolBeer, has also tried to research the concept and invokes Michael Jackson, an award-winning author:

> MJ also mentions that the entire idea of oysters being brewed into stouts may be a myth originating in the pairing of the two separately. Colchester Brewing Company apparently produced an Oyster Feast Stout to celebrate the annual oyster harvest taking place on the River Coine. This was possibly just a regular stout simply named for the occasion, and possibly started the myth. If not, it is the first Oyster Stout on record. It was still produced when Inde Coope and Allsopp took them over in 1925 and was produced under Romford Brewery until at least 1940, according to Michael Ripley of the

Brewers' Society. Regardless, the style became a reality
if it was not already.

Research suggests that oyster shells were used as finings at
one time. Winemakers use eggshells to clarify their wine.
Due to their high alkaline content, oyster shells can work as
a fining agent in the production of beer to counteract the
sourness.

Regardless of oyster stout's genesis, it seems some brewers have taken it to the extreme and are going beyond using
just the shells, introducing whole oysters to the boil. One
doubts that oyster stout will supplant that which is made by
Guinness or Mackeson, but on the artisanal front of beer
making, those tasted are quite pleasant and pair well with
their namesake ingredient.

8
Oysters as an Aphrodisiac

Other foods may be sexy, but none match the oyster for its reputation as an aphrodisiac. Food consumption and human procreation are both primal needs that also bring pleasure, so it is not surprising that the two activities are often connected. There are many languages in which the words for the English verbs 'to copulate' and 'to eat' are very similar. The ancient Greek word *parothides* can be translated as either *hors d'oeuvre* or 'foreplay'. The Kaingang dialect of southern Brazil has a verb which is interchangeably used for either 'copulate' or 'eat' and is only distinguished by a modifier word that specifies 'with the penis' to express which activity is being pursued. In French, the word *consommer* connects concepts of marriages and meals. Food consumption and amorous intent go hand-in-hand with phrases like 'lusty appetites' and 'devouring passions'. The popular Western notion of oysters' ability to increase sexual potency does not, however, extend to China. On the contrary, Meng Shen, a seventh-century pharmacologist, announced that oyster consumption would inhibit nocturnal emissions – literally 'copulation with ghosts and emission of sperm'.

Folklore and superstition play into how certain foods obtain aphrodisiacal status. Historically, a food's influence would be associated with what it resembled. For example, a walnut was believed to strengthen the brain because of its resemblance to an actual human brain, or a banana would cure male impotence because of its phallic shape. Mollusc shells – and particularly oyster shells – have been found by archaeologists in sites that are associated with procreation and are symbolic of the womb, birth and rebirth. The hunter-gatherer societies' use of sympathetic magic as a spiritual exercise to invoke their desires occurred in the form of cave paintings and fetish sculptures. It is believed that cave paintings were created to bring good fortune to a hunt or that the ancients painted images of things they desired. The Ngaro aborigines (Ngaro meaning 'can't see' or 'invisible' in Māori) inhabiting the Whitsunday Islands and coastal regions of Queensland from at least 7000 BC up to their resettlement in the late 1800s are associated with cave openings and nearby mounds, or middens, of oyster shells that are still visible in the steep slopes of Nara Inlet. Their cave paintings – dated to 2,500 years ago – are some of the earliest examples of what may be an attempt to depict the bivalve in artistic form. Although there is no way to determine the intent of these ancient peoples, Mircea Eliade, a famous historian of religions, indicated in his *Images and Symbols* (1961) that 'belief in the magical virtues of oysters and of shells is to be found all over the world, from prehistoric until modern times.' He associated mollusc shells with fertility, because they were given as amulets in various cultures, from the prehistoric Egyptians to nineteenth-century West Africans.

As sexual strength is assumed to generate from foods that resemble a sexual organ, it is no surprise that the oyster is associated with the female nether region. Look at a raw oyster, lying glistening in its freshly opened shell; beckoning to be consumed. In its crude and natural state, it is naked. It is

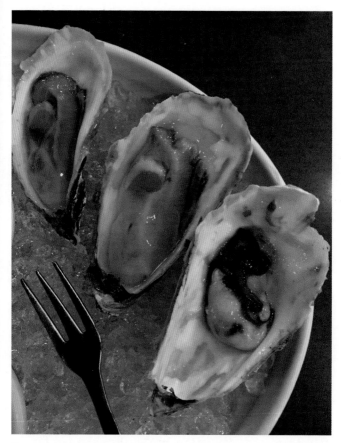

Raw oysters are often compared to the female yoni.

soft and tender. It is inviting and invokes erotic associations like no other food in the world. Akin to a well-endowed woman with extended, fluttery labia – hiding an inner *mons veneris* – the outer edges of a raw oyster might have rippled, grey-tinged tips which accentuate the velvety and rich interior vulva-shaped meat. Still alive – and waiting for its demise – the newly bared oyster gleams under an unctuous liquid of

The goddess of love – known as Aphrodite by the Greeks and Venus by the Romans – is often shown emerging to life from an oyster shell in *The Birth of Venus* by William-Adolphe Bouguereau, *c.* 1879.

uncertainty: is it sweet? Is it salty? Is it creamy? Is it metallic? The uncertainty alone builds trepidation and excitement. The liquor in which the oyster is swimming has an aroma similar to vaginal secretions and is not unlike the most potent female pheromone, TMA (trimethylamine) – luxurious and inviting.

The ancient Greeks' folklore connected oysters with the gods and sex very early on, as displayed in the birth of their goddess of love, Aphrodite. The Romans called her Venus. Aphrodite is often pictured ascending fully formed in delight-ful pulchritudinous glory and ready for copulation on a half shell. According to Hesiod's *Theogony*, the nymph of love was created when Cronus surgically removed Uranus' genitals and threw them into the sea. Thus foam was created, from which Aphrodite appeared. The Greek work *aphros*, from which her name derives, means 'sea foam' and it is from this association that we obtain the word *aphrodisiac*, 'arousing sexual desire'.

Oysters are as associated with male virility as much as female fertility. As this consumable was obligatory at every Roman orgy, many authors of that era penned opinions on their use on the bivalve. Galen of Pergamon, the second-century physician and philosopher – as well as Marcus Aurelius' personal doctor – advised that oysters be consumed as a remedy for declining sexual appetite. Juvenal, the Roman satirist, wrote in his *Satires*, 'Does Venus care about anything when she's drunk? She no longer knows the difference between head and tail, She who laps at giant oysters long, long after midnight' (VI: *The Rites of Bona Dea*). Both Samuel Johnson and William Shakespeare refer to the oysterwench or oysterwoman with connotations of sex or of low moral fortitude.

Artistically, sexual attributes in paintings were symbol-ically portrayed with oysters. Dutch paintings of the seventeenth century commonly depicted oysters in still-life tableaux, evoking qualities of femaleness: both chastity and eroticism, depending on where the oysters appear in the painting and their proximity to other items. If combined with wine, the oyster would be viewed as emblematic of gluttony and lust, but if placed near more common objects such as pewter plates or plain food it would not only symbolize a concealed virtue but suggest that a hidden and desired love was waiting to be revealed. These paintings represent not only the owner's or painter's excellent taste, but sensual pleasure and anticipation. The oysters in many of the still-life artworks of the 1600s and 1700s were the main focus of a painting, often as a moral comment or as a token of erotic intent. In Jan Steen's *A Girl Eating Oysters* (*c.* 1658), the subject is a young girl of obvious wealth as depicted by her garment of lush white fur and velvet. On the table before her is a Delft pitcher and a glass of golden liquid, both expensive items for their era. Also on the table are oysters in various states of shucked and ready-to-eat as well as closed, waiting to be pried apart for consumption. The most remarkable aspect of the painting is the direct and shameless gaze of the subject towards the viewer. It can be interpreted as an invitation to the spectator to join her in her supper, but could also be a beckon towards a sexual interlude.

The very act of shucking an oyster can be looked upon as erotic, as one witnesses deft hands clutching the oyster – cradling and protecting it – while muscled forearms grasp the phallic-shaped knife. Gently probing for the 'secret spot', the union of knifepoint and hinge occurs and with a purposeful thrust, long and hard into the bivalve, the sweetly soft flesh within reveals itself. To consume a raw oyster is to revel in sheer sensuality. Casanova was said to have started each day with a breakfast of fifty oysters, 'off the breasts of a beautiful woman, usually in a warm tub'. In his memoirs he cited

In this Jan Steen painting, *A Girl Eating Oysters, c.* 1658, the girl looking at the viewer is suggestive of an invitation. The addition of the oysters is even more evocative of a sexual interlude.

oysters as 'a spur to the spirit of love' and shared them with
a conquest:

> After making punch we amused ourselves by eating
> oysters, exchanging them when we already had them
> in our mouths. She offered me hers on her tongue at
> the same time that I put mine between her lips; there is
> no more lascivious and voluptuous game between two
> lovers . . . What a sauce that is which dresses an oyster
> I suck from the mouth of the woman I love! It is her
> saliva. The power of love cannot but increase when I
> crush it, when I swallow it.

The sensation of an oyster in one's mouth is visceral; the
head is tilted back and the lips part to accept the ocean's offering. A bit of the salty liquor precedes the entry of the fleshy,
soft meat – greeting the tongue and sliding back towards the
throat. Does one gently bite into the oyster's whole body and
hope to prolong the sensation by breaking up the stimulating
morsel? All I know is that all those years ago, with my Aunt
Lola in New Orleans, my twelve-year-old mouth felt alive as
I was initiated into adulthood; accepted into the a cabal of
sensualists with the taste of that first oyster.

The eighteenth century – in France specifically – was the
pinnacle of historical debauchery and promiscuity as attested
by the likes of Casanova. It was an era that was freeing itself
from medieval superstition and Church rule. Liquors becoming more prevalent, accompanied by the lowering of inhib-
itions, brought about the rise of sensual, physical pleasure.
This Age of Reason established the building blocks of our
modern society and civilization through scientific discovery,
physical pleasure and literary expression. Leading the way
as both Sun King to his country and the monarch of excess

was Louis XIV of France, who made oysters fashionable at the court of Versailles by his mandatory diet of daily oysters from the emerald-coloured French coast of Cancale. Voltaire, Diderot and Rousseau, leaders of the Enlightenment philosophical movement in France, were all convinced that an increased libido helped to inspire creative intellectual thought and that the consumption of oysters would assist in this profound endeavour. After the removal of the French monarchy, the imperial Bonapartes were as enamoured with the bivalve as the royalty they overthrew. Many of Napoleon's enemies claimed that the Little General would have to eat oysters before a battle, which may explain why both Danton and Robespierre are reputed to have consumed several dozen when their ideologies failed them. It is believed that Napoleon's sister Pauline returned to Europe from her exile in Santo Domingo with a handful of African slaves whose sole duty was to do her bidding. Notable among them was a well-endowed man whose daily task was to carry Pauline to her morning bath and feed her a breakfast of fresh oysters and champagne. One can only speculate that his services involved more than shucking oysters and serving food.

Brothels and oyster houses go hand-in-hand, contributing to the affiliation of oysters and sex. The first 'red-light district' dates back to fourteenth-century Amsterdam, mostly catering to sailors, therein connecting sex with seafood. But nineteenth-century New York City's red-light district was in the Bowery and the place to dine upon oysters was in cellar restaurants, often situated underneath or next to brothels. In his *American Notes* (1842), Charles Dickens (believed to have enlisted the amorous services of one Julia Brown) commented upon the plethora of sketchy dance halls and the oyster restaurants which were located semi-underground and had to be marked with red lights:

It is said that the consumption of oysters can help one's libido.

These signs which are so plentiful, in shape like river buoys, or small balloons, hoisted by cords to poles, and dangling there, announce, as you may see by looking up, 'Oysters in Every Style.' They tempt the hungry most at night, for then dull candles glimmering inside, illuminate these dainty words, and make the mouths of idlers water, as they read and linger.

Of these New York locales, author George G. Foster wrote in his *New York By Gas-light* (1850), 'the women were all of one kind, but the oysters came in a variety of types.'

The phenomenon of brothels being associated with oyster clubs was hardly limited to New York. In 1850, on the other side of the continent, the city of San Diego became part of the United States with the admission of California to the Union following the Mexican–American War. San Diego's denizens of distraction were housed in the Stingaree District where there was a well-known brothel named the Golden Poppy owned by Madam Cora, situated upstairs from the city's most popular gambling hall and saloon, The Oyster Bar. Madam Cora may have owned the brothel, but the saloon's owner was none other than Wyatt Earp, who took part in the gunfight at the O. K. Corral. The Golden Poppy was famous for decorating its rooms and ladies in matching colours, and customers would arrive and gain fortitude with a dozen or so oysters before choosing their companions. With a precedent set, it is no surprise that Hugh Hefner placed his New Orleans club in between the two and across the street from very well-established oyster bars. Even the mere concept of *The Oyster* (and *The Pearl*) was utilized by William Lazenby as the titles for his now-infamous erotic monthly magazines published in London from 1879 to 1880.

On a more practical level, modern science is now verifying many of the historical aphrodisiacal claims. Oysters are rich in zinc, a known mineral that will aid male virility. The prostrate needs ten times more zinc than any other organ in the body, secreting one to three milligrams per ejaculation. In March 2005 a joint study by American and Italian scientists announced that there is some validity to the mythology of an oyster as aphrodisiac. In their study, a process called high-performance liquid chromatography was used to pinpoint two specific amino acids present in oysters: D-aspartic acid (D-Asp) and N-methyl-D-aspartate (NMDA). These amino acids injected into rats produce an increase of testosterone in the male rats and progesterone in the female rats, both of which also increase libido. Oysters also contain dopamine, a neurotransmitter which assists the brain in the governance and activity of sexual desire in both men and women. But cooking greatly reduces the amount of D-Asp and NMDA molecules, so consuming the oysters raw is preferable for those with amorous intentions.

9
The Future of Oysters

The oyster of the future will be very much like the ones trodden upon by dinosaurs millions of years ago and the ones we eat today – yet it will be remarkably different. Our humble bivalve has been the human race's longest continuously exploited food source. As such, there are many who are working hard to insure against its endangerment. We live in a world of genetically modified foods and the oyster is no different in that regard. The average consumer may never realize they are eating an oyster that has been manipulated in some fashion. We have been witness to several diseases that have decimated oyster beds and scientists continue to work hard to find ways to keep this from happening.

One method to fight recurring disease is to try and grow varieties of edible oyster that are not well known on the marketplace. For example, the Chinese river oyster (*Crassostrea ariakensis*) is found in rivers in Japan, China, India and Pakistan. Some hatcheries on the West Coast of America are experimenting with them as a replacement for the Pacific oyster during spawning summer months. This Chinese river oyster had proven itself to be disease-resistant and faster growing. There was a valiant effort by some Virginia aquaculturists to bring the species to the Chesapeake, but after study and debate it was ultimately deemed too risky. One of the biggest issues with transplanting one oyster to a new region is the unintentional consequence of other invasive species hitching a ride, thriving in new territories and wreaking havoc. That is what happened to some Japanese seed shipments that unknowingly brought along a little parasite known as an oyster drill (*Ceratostoma inornatum*) that was damaging to newly seeded oyster crops.

Scientists have been working on strengthening the oyster's longevity with a modification known as the triploid. Ordinary oysters are considered diploids in that during reproduction, the egg and the sperm each contribute one set of chromosomes. Scientists construct triploid oysters using two sets of chromosomes from the egg and one from the sperm. The resulting triploid has three sets of chromosomes in total, making it reproductively sterile. By manipulating and controlling these basic reproductive functions, the scientists are creating an oyster that has no spawning season. Proponents believe there is little difference in flavour and the public at large may have no idea that they are eating a triploid oyster. In 2009 more than 8 billion triploid larvae were hatched.

Another scientific advancement imposed upon oysters is that of irradiation. Irradiated food is not a new concept. Patents were first issued in 1905 to improve the shelf life of foods by reducing or eliminating microorganisms through ionization. In the 1950s, the U.S. military expanded its experiments and use of irradiation on produce, meats and dairy products, but it was Russia and Canada that were the first countries to irradiate potatoes and wheat for public consumption. By the late 1980s, the process saw a more widespread commercialization. In oysters, irradiation is used to kill the bacteria *Vibrio vulnificus*, which – although harmless to the oyster – can cause severe gastrointestinal illness in humans. The irradiation process

Modern Chinese bamboo raft farming.

effectively kills the deadly microbe but also kills the living oyster and exponentially shortens its shelf life. After effectively 'pre-shucking' the oyster – the process separates the adductor muscle from its shell – the oysters are then wrapped in a yellow rubber band to keep them closed. This type of oysters is found in the casino and cruise ship industries where high volumes of oysters need to be prepared and served daily. Advocates of the practice claim it is a good option for those who suffer from liver disease or a compromised immune system. Distributors can sell them to restaurants who can't afford the skilled shucking labour, but because the oyster is no longer alive, the flavours begin to dull, the texture becomes mushy and there is less freshness and vibrancy. This is another reason to inquire about the tag or watch your oysters being shucked at an oyster bar: to ensure they are fresh and still alive.

Are you curious why there seem to be so many new types of oysters these days? Chalk that up to the artisan grower and those who are creating new oysters. The growers I met in Carlsbad are a perfect example. On the California coast, about an hour's drive north of San Diego, is a small lagoon that sits in the shadow of an old power plant where no oyster had ever naturally grown. But abalone farmer John Davis saw the potential and brought scientist Dennis Peterson in to establish oysters. The advantage is that the power plant keeps the lagoon naturally dredged and the altered environment helps produce a natural and healthy ecosystem.

Utilizing *affinage*, one of the finishing steps taken to create a better tasting oyster is to tumble oysters during their growing process. Carlsbad Aquafarm is doing this with two different oysters, *C. gigas* for their Carlsbad Blonde, and an Olympia oyster, the Carlsbad Luna. Similar oysters using this process include the Kusshi and the Old 1871 oyster. The tumbling spins the oysters around and chips away bits of the edge of the outer shell, enabling the oysters to grow deeper instead of wider. Nature might have made a flatter, thinner oyster,

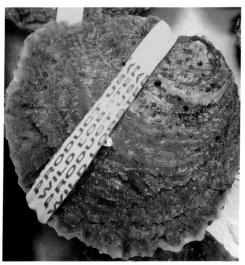

The dreaded yellow-banded oyster, avoided by true oyster connoisseurs.

This tumbler is used in the process of *affinage*, which gently tumbles the oysters to break off the edges, thereby causing a deeper bowl with more liquor.

but this level of control for a grower can create a rounder, meatier and fleshier oyster with more liquor. Oysters are like wine. In wine, one can taste the 'terroir' of where a wine grape has been grown. With oysters, one tastes the 'merroir' of where it has lived – its environment that includes how salty the water was, the water's varying temperatures, and the ebbs and flows of the tide that streamed through the oyster's existence.

From the demise of the nineteenth-century oyster, we have an opportunity to rebuild the oyster as not only a viable, edible food source, but a keystone species in the restoration of damaged ecosystems. Each individual oyster can filter up to 190 litres (50 gallons) of water per day. Healthy oyster beds are demonstrably beneficial to the environment as these hard-working bivalves improve water quality by cycling water, an act that is critical to coastal restoration, especially in places like the Gulf of Mexico where the BP oil spill occurred in

2010. Initiatives such as Living Breakwaters and the Billion Oyster Project, both based in New York, are introducing oysters back into the New York Harbor and the South Shore of Staten Island, respectively, to help revive ecologies in severely polluted, damaged waters. Schoolchildren are even getting involved in the care of these newly formed estuaries to help monitor the change in water quality. The students are not only learning hands-on scientific research but are taking stewardship of their future and their potential future resources. The Living Breakwaters programme is helping to create reefs of non-edible oysters that will reduce the impact of

A contemporary oyster plate.

A first-time oyster eater.

devastating tidal surges like Hurricane Sandy in 2012. In effect, an 'oyster dam' could ultimately save lives.

Brent Petkau, 'The Oyster Man', explains,

> We are living in an age where eating food is a very political act. I, in a very small way, can grab a bull by the horns and present an oyster to the world as an experience that is second to none. It is *the* sustainable seafood source for the future. It can provide another type of food with accountability. You can trust the oyster grower because there is accountability. I grow an oyster and present it to the marketplace. If it is not clean and healthy, there will be a phone call the next day. There is a connection between eating the food and knowing where it is grown. So I will give the world an oyster.

In doing so, perhaps the oyster will save our planet and mankind.

Oysterman Brent Petkau uses traditional methods to raise, cultivate and produce oysters.

Buying, Storing and Shucking Oysters

Oysters are alive when they are pulled from the waters and should remain alive from the day they are harvested, through the time they are transported to the seller to the moment they are opened and slipped into one's mouth or cooking vessel. Once pulled from the water, with proper handling, an oyster can stay alive for up to four weeks. Obviously fresher is better. When harvesters bag the oysters for shipment, a tag is slapped to the bag to identify some basic information, most notably 'harvest date' and 'location'. Other information includes licensing, shipping and other legal information. The harvest date is what is important to the consumer and guarantees you are getting a fresh oyster. Inspect your oyster; you do not want one with shell damage that may expose the oyster within. Avoid any that have open gaps. Ideally, an oyster out of water has spent its time with the cup side down, so that the meat of the flesh remains in its own liquor and does not dry out. If you are not going to open your oysters immediately, they can be stored in your refrigerator for up to a week. Store them cup-side down, wrapped in a damp towel. Re-moisten your towel as needed until you are ready to shuck them. As oysters are alive, you want to do everything you can to keep them that way until they are consumed. They are delicate creatures that require care. This includes not putting them in a freezer, not storing them in so much ice that the ice melts and 'drowns them' in fresh water, and not letting them dry out.

Opening an oyster is easy – most of the time. It is an intimidating process and every now and then a particularly strong or hidden hinge, or especially tight adductor muscle, can stump even the most skilful shuckers. One must have proper tools, a practised technique and perseverance. The tools include a properly shaped shucking knife and appropriate hand protection, be it gloves or a heavy towel. Because the oyster is a wet creature with a very hard shell, the moisture can cause slippage so it is very easy to injure oneself. Be patient and careful, and above all, protect your hands. Do not try to use a kitchen butter knife, a screwdriver, a hammer or any old sharp kitchen knife. Standard butter knives are too flimsy, with a rounded tip that will not be able to access the hinge and a handle that is not strong enough for the force that is required. A screwdriver has too blunt and thick a tip to adequately access the hinge, and no flat edge to slice through the adductor muscle. Those small, sharp paring knives are also too flimsy and weak and it will be too easy to slip and cut yourself. The shucker's knife needs to be of good quality with a sturdy blade that will not bend easily. Most have been carefully made to come to a sharp point. A good knife will fit firmly and snuggly in your hand without slipping and the point will be thin and strong enough to penetrate the toughest shells.

I cannot reiterate enough how important it is to protect your hands because it is so easy for the knife to slip and this explains why most shuckers wear gloves. There are many good-quality gloves on the market that range in price from $10 to $300 (£8 to £250). The more expensive ones are made of chainmail and would only be needed by professionals who shuck oysters for hours at a time. For a very reasonable price,

Protective gloves are the stock-and-trade of oyster shuckers, and there are a variety of knives available on the market.

look for those that are constructed of Kevlar and coated latex as these are considered 'slash-resistant' but are still flexible enough for handling the delicate oysters. If not wearing gloves, a thick dishcloth will protect your hands.

Lay the oyster with the cup side down as you want to try and reserve as much of the interior liquor as possible. Some will always get spilled so don't worry about that too much. The entire procedure should be done with the oyster remaining completely horizontal at all times. The intention is to keep the oyster and its lower shell as undamaged as possible.

Insert the knife just to the edge of the hinge. While simultaneously inserting the knife into the hinge, provide a gentle twisting motion. You might hear a slight, wet popping sound. This is to release the top, flatter shell away from the larger shell that is holding the oyster and the liquor.

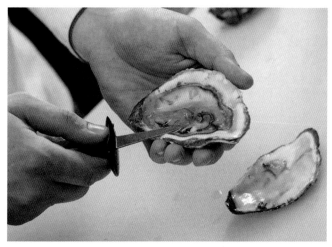

Gently twist until you hear the adductor muscle 'pop' open, then gently fold back the upper shell to reveal the inner oyster.

Carefully run the edge of the knife up along the top inside edge of the upper-most shell. This action is to sever the adductor muscle from the oyster.

Briefly run the knife under the oyster to release it from the larger shell, taking care to retain as much of the liquid as possible. Many professional shuckers will use this opportunity to flip the oyster over. A few shards of shell might be dislodged in the oyster cavity. Just flick those out with your knife before service. It is best to have a platter of crushed ice available to nestle the opened oysters before service. If you are planning on cooking the oysters, I find salt or a bowl of old beans or rice is a good makeshift alternative.

Many are happy with their oysters just opened raw, on the half shell, with a squeeze of lemon or a splash of mignonette.

Recipes

A true aficionado prefers the oyster raw, on the half shell, with little or no adornment. A first-timer may be frightened of a raw oyster and will shy away from something 'gross', 'icky' or 'slimy'. In truth, a really fresh oyster will never be slimy. Go ahead and smell a freshly shucked oyster. There will be a hint of the delight of the ocean in the aroma. It should not be an odour of dead or rotting fish. If it smells bad or pungent, discard it. First try an unadulterated oyster without any toppings. If you think you need all the sauce, you will not get all the true flavours of the oyster itself – you will taste nothing but sauce. As Louis P. De Gouy stated in his masterful cookbook *The Oyster Book* (containing 266 recipes!): 'The dunkers-in-catsup are probably not aware that oysters from different beds, even beds situated in the same body of water not many miles apart, have definitely different tastes.' Try a small one first: a tiny Kumamoto or a Malpeque (an Olympia) – you *can* get through it and there *will* be a sensation of accomplishment. Do not swallow your food whole! Chew a little to release the flavour and then swallow. There is a sweetness that will stay with you, haunt you. It will beckon you to return.

If trying them for the first time, a squeeze of lemon might help. No matter where in the world raw oysters are served, it is always accompanied by sliced lemons or occasionally limes. The clean, creamy, salty oyster can be complemented with the bright acidity of the citrus juice, but in moderation, please.

Other Garnishes

Besides plain lemon, there are other traditional garnishes served with oysters – and many non-traditional toppings. Mignonette sauce is the one that comes to mind first.

100 g (4 oz) good quality red wine vinegar
1 medium-sized shallot, finely minced
1 tsp freshly cracked black pepper

Mix ingredients together in a shallow bowl and allow to sit for at least an hour to macerate the shallots before dribbling some into your oyster.

Cocktail sauce is another accompaniment that will be offered with oysters on the half shell. Many will buy a bottled cocktail sauce, but if you want to make your own, these are easy ingredients to combine:

35 g (¼ cup) tomato ketchup
1 to 2 tbsp prepared horseradish, to taste
2 tsp lemon juice
Worcestershire sauce and Tabasco sauce to taste

There are some oyster bars that will offer all of the above ingredients separately and allow the diner to blend together or use any one of them singularly on their oysters. Incomprehensibly, there are many people who enjoy pure horseradish on their oyster. In America, a few drops of Tabasco on an oyster before letting it slip into your mouth is quite popular. To give your oysters an Asian flare, any number of Japanese, Chinese or Vietnamese dipping sauces can be used. In Japan, a classic *ponzu* sauce is made from the following:

4 tbsp soy sauce
2 tbsp rice vinegar (*mirin*)
2 tbsp citrus juice (lemon or yuzu)

Koreans usually eat raw oysters with *gochujang* sauce (고추장, pungent fermented Korean condiment made from red chili, glutinous rice, fermented soybeans and salt) or salted sesame oil. Throughout Korea, there is a preponderance of late-night drinking establishments that will grill or steam oysters to accompany the cocktail.

Nước chấm is a Vietnamese dipping sauce that is based on bottled fish sauce available from speciality markets:

2 tbsp Vietnamese fish sauce
4 tbsp lime juice
1 small garlic clove, finely minced
2 tsp granulated sugar
120 ml (½ cup) hot water
Thai chilli, minced and added to taste

As with all these sauce offerings, the ingredients and measurements are not exact and the oyster lends itself to experimentation and playfulness! Try a bit of caviar or a slice of *uni* (sea urchin) as another accompaniment.

Oyster Shooters

An 'oyster shooter' is an alcoholic beverage that contains an oyster. There is one story similar to that of the Hangtown Fry whereby a gold miner in California in 1860 stumbles into a saloon and orders a plate of oysters, cocktail sauce and a shot of whiskey. Dumping them all into the glass together and swallowing it in one fell swoop, the barkeep asks, 'What sort of mess do you call that?' To which the miner responds, 'I call that an oyster cocktail.' Legend has it that the saloon put up a sign the next day: 'Oyster Cocktail – Four Bits Per Glass.' While a classic cocktail is sipped and savoured, a 'shooter' is a neologism for a mixed drink that can be consumed in one swallow. The idea of slipping an oyster into alcohol for consumption seems to have fallen by the wayside from the days of our California miner, until the cocktail culture of the 1970s made bars and lounges social scenes. Many variations of the oyster shooter are similar to a Bloody Mary with the addition of an oyster:

dash of red Tabasco
dash of green Tabasco
dash of horseradish
30 ml (1 oz) vodka
1 freshly shucked oyster
lemon slice

Combine all liquid ingredients in a cocktail shaker with ice, shake vigorously and strain into a shot glass. Add oyster and serve.

Many Japanese restaurants are offering their version of oyster shooters with *sake*. A creative mixologist can go light or heavy with their use of Japanese ingredients, using just *sake*, a bit of *mirin* and diced cucumber for a light offering, but I am fond of this variation that includes a quail egg for a more substantial *amuse-bouche*:

30 ml (1 oz) dry *sake*
1 tsp rice wine vinegar (*mirin*)
1 tsp soy sauce
1 freshly shucked oyster
1 quail egg
tobiko to garnish

Blend the sake, vinegar and soy sauce. Place oyster in a Japanese soup spoon, top with raw quail egg, blended ingredients and garnish with *tobiko*.

Beverage Pairings

The classic beverage pairing with oysters is champagne. The light, clean effervescent bubbles help brighten and cleanse the palate. Some wines can overpower the taste of the oyster; those high in acidity or tannins can conflict with the oyster, causing them to taste sour or even more salty. The French pairing of sancerre or muscadet dates back to the 1880s. These are wines from the Loire Valley, which is near the city of Nantes on the Atlantic. The wines are known for their crisp, citrus flavours countered with earthy and mineral aromatics that make for a refreshing offering. There has been speculation that these wines date back to Roman times, which is why they have such a long-standing history with oysters. An American or Australian alternative to these French wines would be sauvignon blanc or pinot blanc. They are similar in profile to the French wines – a bit austere with a touch of citrus. Chardonnays are more robust white wines and I think their oaky, buttery qualities coat the tongue when eating oysters and conflict with the subtle, elegant flavours the bivalve has to offer.

The quintessential Brazilian experience is to squeeze lime on to your oysters and pair them with a Caipirinha cocktail. Comprised of cachaça (a distilled spirit made from sugar cane, not unlike white rum) and muddled limes, this is a very refreshing, citrusy cocktail that will not overpower the oysters – especially since many in Brazil prefer to squeeze lime onto their oysters instead of lemon. The Russians consume their raw oysters with caviar and vodka. Along the Adriatic Sea or the Mediterranean, expect to see anise-flavoured liquors such as *arak* in Turkey or *ouzo* in Greece being served with their raw oysters. The French artist Henri de Toulouse-Lautrec accompanied his oysters on the half shell with the French version of the anise-flavoured liquor, absinthe, which has had a resurgence and is now available in many countries. The Japanese enjoy their oysters with *sake* or beer. If drinking *sake*, consider one that is dryer, versus the unfiltered, sweeter *sake* that will overpower the oyster. Again, oysters on the half shell, when accompanied by a hearty stout with rustic brown bread and butter, is also exceptional.

On Buying Pre-shucked Oysters

Most American supermarkets carry jars of pre-shucked oysters in their fresh fish section and British supermarkets sell them frozen. In Japan, they come in sausage-shaped tubes in liquid. All of these are a good alternative for stews, soups or other recipes where the oyster is cooked. The liquid in the jar is not oyster juice, as is often thought. It is clean water that is used to rinse the shucked oysters. That liquid will not add much flavour to a dish but I will sometimes add it 'just in case', especially to stews or soups where an extra addition of oyster flavour can only better a dish. Regardless, do strain the liquid and examine the oysters for bits of shells that might remain. The sizes of these pre-shucked oysters vary, so opening the package is akin to opening a gift; one never knows how many one will get or how big they will be. They can be as large as 7 to 10 cm (3 to 4 in.) in length, in which case, trim the oysters down to a consistent, mouth-feel size, about the size of a shelled walnut. Do not consume jarred or frozen oysters without cooking them first.

Chinese Oyster Sauce – Made Two Ways

Note that home-made oyster sauce contains soy sauce while most of the jarred brands do not, but those contain many additional ingredients such as protein additives, sodium benzoate and yeast extracts.

First Sauce:
600 ml (1 pint) oysters, with liquor
80 ml (⅓ cup) of water
3 tbsp soy sauce

Pestle and mortar the oysters into a paste, reserving the liquid. Bring the oyster paste and water to a boil and reduce and simmer for half an hour, or until thickened and dark. Sieve the mixture and reserve the solids (can be used in an omelette or soup for flavouring). Add the soy sauce and remaining oyster liquor. This can be refrigerated for up to one week.

Second Sauce:
1.2 litres (2 pints) oysters with liquor, very finely diced
120 ml (½ cup) chicken stock
2 tbsp Shaoxing wine or dry sherry
3 tbsp soy sauce
1 tsp sugar
1 tsp corn oil

Bring oysters, chicken stock and wine to a boil and then reduce to simmer for ten to fifteen minutes. Add the remaining ingredients and continue to simmer for an additional ten minutes. Strain the mixture (reserving the oysters for use in an omelette or soup). Sauce can be refrigerated for up to one week.

Historical Recipes

Oysters (First Century, Roman)
from Apicius, late fourth to fifth century AD

To oysters, which want to be well seasoned, add pepper, lovage, yolks, vinegar, broth, oil and wine; if you wish also add honey.

Stewed Oysters (British, 1654)
from Joseph Cooper, chief cook to the late king (Charles I), *The Art of Cookery Refin'd and Augmented*

Straine the liquor from the Oysters, then wash them very clean, and put them into a pipkin with the liquor, a pinte of Wine to a quart of Oysters, two or three whole Onions, large Mace, Pepper, Ginger; let all the spices be whole, they will stew the whiter; put in Salt, a little Vinegar, a piece of butter and sweet Herbs; stew all these together till you think them enough, then take out some of that liquor and put to it a quarter of a pound of butter, a Lemon minced, and beat it up thick, setting it on the fire, but let it not boyle; dreine the rest of the liquor from the Oysters thorow a culender, and dish them; pour this sauce over them; garnish your dish with searced Ginger, Lemmon, Orange, Barberries, or Grapes scalded; sippit it, and serve it up.

Oyster Loaves (British, 1730)
from Edward Kidder's *Receipt of Pastry and Cookery – for use of his scholars*

Like many 'cookbooks' of the era, no actual measurements are given. As these recipes were for fellow students, it was assumed they would know common techniques and proportions. Subsequent variations of the oyster loaf recipe appear in practically every cookbook that utilizes oysters for the next two hundred years.

Cut a round hole in the tops of 5 french
Roals & take out all the crumb & smear them
Over the sides with a tender forcd meat made
Of set oysters part of an Eele pistastia
Nuts mushrooms herbs anchovys marrow
Spice the yolks of 2 hard eggs beat these
Well in a mortar with one raw egg then fry
Them crisp in lard & fill them with a qt. of oysters the
Rest of the Eele cut like lard spice
Mushrooms anchovys tossed up in their
Liquor ½ a pt. of white sine thicken it with
Eggs & a bitt of butter rould up in flower

Shoulder of Mutton with Oysters (British, 1730)

from Charles Carter's *Complete Practical Book*; this was a favourite of Charles Dickens

First take your Oysters, and set them, and beard them; then take some Parsley, Thyme, Pepper, Salt, and some crumb'd Bread; mix all these well together; then take the Yolks of four Eggs; mix up your Oysters in all this; then raise a few Holes, and stuff your Mutton with three Oysters in a Hole; then cover with a Mutton Caul, and so roast it gently: Garnish with Mutton Cutlets.

Kamenica (Croatian Grilled Oysters)

It was the Croatians who helped boost the Gulf Coast oyster industry and this is a classic version brought from home:

16 g (⅛ cup) grated Parmesan cheese
16 g (⅛ cup) grated Romano cheese
225 g (8 oz) butter, softened
oregano and black pepper to taste
1 tbsp finely chopped garlic
2 tbsp flat-leaf parsley, finely chopped
12 large oysters, shucked, on their shells with liquor

Mix the grated cheeses together and set aside. In a bowl or mixer, blend together the butter, garlic, parsley and ground pepper. Heat a charcoal or gas grill and carefully place the oysters onto the hottest part of the grill and scoop a tablespoon of the blended butter onto the oyster. When the oyster has plumped, the liquor and butter will bubble over a bit, about five minutes. Sprinkle with reserved cheese and serve immediately with crusty French bread.

Hangtown Fry (American, 1849)

Besides Oyster Rockefeller, the Hangtown Fry is the most famous oyster recipe in history. Like the Rockefeller, the Hangtown Fry – with its special combination of fried oysters, bacon and eggs – comes with its own legend. It definitely originated with the California Gold Rush of 1849 in a little area about 200 km (130 mi.) east of San Francisco. James W. Marshall discovered the first nugget of gold at Sutter's Mill in January of 1848 and by 1849 more than 300,000 people descended upon the area in search of gold. All these people scattered about and created a handful of dry, rugged and untamed mining camps that slowly turned into small communities. In a form of outrageous one-upmanship, camps were given different names like 'Dry Diggins', 'Hard-up Gulch' and 'Humbug Flat'. 'Hangtown' was a camp that earned its moniker because of the numerous hangings that occurred there. After striking a rich vein of gold, one legend has the prospector stomping into the Cary House Hotel, plunking down a bag of gold nuggets and ordering the most expensive dish possible. Because of the hotel's remote location, the three most expensive ingredients were eggs (which had to come from Farallon Island gull birds – not chickens as they do now – located an additional 32 km (20 mi.) in the ocean beyond San Francisco), bacon (which was shipped in from the East Coast via pack mules or around Cape Horn) and our precious oyster, also from the San Francisco harbour, carefully packed in expensive ice for the journey. The dish earned such notoriety that it quickly appeared on menus along the Pacific Coast and was listed as a members-only breakfast option at the famed New York 21 Club.

The other legend is similarly grandiose and involves a miner who got into a squabble with another prospector over a gold claim. An argument ensued, guns were drawn and soon a man was dead. The convicted murderer, waiting his turn in Hangtown for the noose, was asked what he wanted for his last meal. He could postpone his demise by asking for a dish that would require several days – if not longer – to obtain the ingredients. This recipe can be easily doubled for two people but is a hearty breakfast for one:

30 g (¼ cup) breadcrumbs
35 g (¼ cup) flour
4 eggs
4 shucked oysters
2 tbsp butter
2 strips cooked bacon, crumbled
1 spring onion (scallion), thinly sliced
salt and pepper to taste

In separate bowls, place the breadcrumbs, flour and one egg, slightly beaten. Gently whisk remaining eggs and keep in reserve. Pat the oysters dry and dip each one, consecutively, in flour, then egg, then breadcrumbs and reserve on a separate plate. Heat butter in a 20 cm (8 in.) skillet over medium heat and gently fry the oysters until golden brown, one to two minutes per side, being careful not to over-cook them. Add the eggs, scrambling gently. After a minute or two – when the eggs are beginning to set – add the spring onion and bacon. Continue to cook until eggs are set, about four to five minutes. Transfer omelette to a plate and serve. In California, this is often served with Tabasco sauce.

Mrs Beeton's Oyster Soup (1861)

6 dozen oysters
1,900 ml (2 quarts) white stock
300 ml (½ pint) cream
2 tbsp butter
1 ½ tbsp flour
salt, cayenne and mace to taste

Scald the oysters in their own liquor; take them out, beard them and put them in a tureen. Take a pint of the stock, put in the beards and the liquor, which must be carefully strained, and simmer for half an hour. Take it off the fire, strain it again and add the remainder of the stock with the seasoning and mace. Bring it to a boil, add the thickening of butter and flour, simmer for five minutes, stir in the boiling cream, pour it over the oysters and serve.

Note: This soup can be made less rich by using milk instead of cream, and thickening with arrowroot instead of butter and flour.

Oyster Patties
Jennie June, *American Cookery Book* (1870)

Beard the oysters, and, if large, halve them; put them into a saucepan with a piece of butter rolled in flour, some finely shredded lemon rind, and a little white pepper, and milk, and a portion of the liquor from the fish; stir all well together, let simmer for a few minutes, and put it in your patty pans [akin to shallow cupcake pans], which should already be prepared with puff paste in the usual way. Serve hot or cold.

Oysters Favourite (*Huîtres à la favorite*)
August Escoffier, 1903

Poach the oysters bearded in their own liquor, which should have been carefully collected when opening them. Clean their hollow shells, and place them on a tray covered with a layer of rock salt one-half-inch thick. Garnish them with Béchamel sauce; upon the latter, in each shell, lay an oyster decorated with a slice of truffle; cover with the same sauce; sprinkle with grated Parmesan cheese and melted butter, and set to glaze quickly. Serve immediately.

Oyster Stuffing (America, *c.* 1920s)

Americans have been stuffing turkeys with oysters since arriving on the country's shores in the 1600s. Originally, home cooks would fill their turkeys and other birds with oysters to stretch the pricier fowl. Now it is oysters that are more expensive and make the addition of an oyster stuffing more of a special occasion. To honour the heritage of my husband's Jewish ancestors, I offer his great-grandmother's *treyf*-based recipe:

65 g (½ cup) celery, diced
65 g (½ cup) onion, diced
110 g (½ cup) melted butter
600 ml (1 pint) oysters, or as many shucked oysters to measure approximately 250 ml (1 cup), finely chopped
200 g (4 cups) breadcrumbs or lightly toasted bread cut into cubes
1 small garlic clove, minced
20 g (¼ cup) chopped fresh parsley
60–120 ml (¼–½ cup) oyster liquor
1 tsp powdered ginger
1 tsp white pepper
250 ml (1 cup) chicken stock
1 egg
salt

Sauté the onions and celery in four tablespoons butter until limp. Add chopped oysters until lightly cooked. Add herbs, spices, garlic and breadcrumbs until all ingredients are well coated and transfer to large bowl. Add the remaining melted butter and oyster broth, chicken broth or water until combined and moist, but not compressed. Place in bird while moist and bake as directed. Alternately, stuffing may be placed in well-buttered casserole dish and baked at 180°C (350°F) degrees until heated through with a light brown crust, approximately thirty minutes.

Oyster Rockefeller

There are many versions of Oysters Rockefeller. They must contain some green ingredient although there is considerable debate if the green is spinach or not. Some say there must always be cheese while others would never use cheese. Here are two versions:

Place oysters on a half shell in preheated deep dishes filled with sand (silver sand glistens prettily). Cover the oysters thickly with ¼ chopped parsley, ¼ finely chopped raw spinach, ⅛ finely chopped tarragon, ⅛ finely chopped chervil, ⅛ finely chopped basil and ⅛ finely chopped chives. Salt and pepper some fresh breadcrumbs, cover the herbs completely, dot with melted butter and put for 4 or 5 minutes in a preheated 450° oven. Serve piping hot. This dish is an enormous success with French gourmets. It makes more friends for the United States than anything I knew.

A Tried and True Method

1 rib celery, finely diced
2 green onions, minced
110 g (¼ lb) butter
150 g (2 cups) spinach, finely chopped
75 g (1 cup) watercress, finely chopped
50 g (½ cup) dried breadcrumbs
2 tbsp Pernod or other anise-flavoured liquor
dash of Tabasco
dash of Worcestershire sauce
25 g (¼ cup) grated Parmesan cheese
24 oysters on the half shell
1 lemon, quartered
rock salt or crumpled aluminum foil

Pre-heat broiler to 230°C (450°F). Sauté green onions and celery in butter until tender. Add chopped spinach and watercress and cook for one minute; remove from heat. Stir in the remainder of the ingredients except for the cheese. Spread rock salt over a large baking dish and arrange the oysters in their half shell on top of the salt. Top each oyster with a teaspoon of the mixture and sprinkle a little cheese on top. Bake for eight to ten minutes until hot and bubbly. Serve immediately with lemon garnish.

Variations include adding a little cooked bacon or a slice of chorizo under the sauce, or alternatively not using any cheese at all and topping the oyster with more breadcrumbs and a small dollop of butter, shallots instead of green onions, etc. It is an easy recipe to experiment with!

Hoi Tod
(Thai omelette with oysters; typically,
a small dish that is enjoyed all day long)

2 tbsp rice flour
1 tsp fried chicken batter (cassava starch)
½ tsp cornstarch
3 tbsp very cold water
2 tbsp chopped green onion
600 ml (1 pint) jarred oysters
60 g (1 cup) fresh beansprouts, rinsed
¼ tsp chopped garlic
¼ tsp soy sauce
1 egg
vegetable oil for cooking
¼ tsp Thai pepper powder

Mix the first three ingredients, then add cold water and mix well. Add one tablespoon of the chopped onion to your batter, then add oysters. Pour this into your lightly oiled, preheated wok or non-stick pan. Keep moving the oysters around for a minute or two to cook them evenly. Crack an egg over the middle of the *hoi tod*, and scramble briefly. Let this cook for three minutes; it needs to turn golden brown on the underside.

Flip your *hoi tod*, and let it cook for another two minutes. Push your *hoi tod* to the side of your pan, and add some chopped garlic to the pan. Add the beansprouts to the garlic and stir to combine, for just a minute, adding a bit of soy sauce to the sprouts as they cook. Scoop up your sprouts and put on your plate, then put the *hoi tod* over the sprouts. Sprinkle with Thai pepper powder, the remaining spring onions, and serve it with Thai sweet chilli sauce or Sriracha sauce.

Oysters with Pancetta and Leeks over Fettuccine

A quick and easy way to showcase the oyster and make an elegant presentation.

100 g (4 oz) pancetta, julienne sliced
3 tbsp butter
2 leeks, thinly sliced
225 g (½ lb) oyster mushrooms, sliced
1 garlic clove, minced
2 sprigs fresh thyme
2 tbsp lemon juice
125 ml (½ cup) dry white wine
600 ml (1 pint) shucked oysters; liquor reserved
250 ml (1 cup) heavy cream
fresh parsley for garnish
salt and pepper to taste
Parmigiano cheese for garnish
225 g (½ lb) fettuccine noodles

Heat a 30 cm (12 in.) pan over medium heat and sauté the pancetta until crispy. Add the butter until melted and toss in the leeks and mushrooms until limp, two to three minutes. Add the garlic, thyme, lemon juice and wine. Bring to a boil and add reserved oyster liquor. Bring to a boil again and reduce by half. Add cream and reduce until slightly thickened. Finally, add the oysters and cook for only two or three minutes, until warmed through. Add salt and pepper to taste. Serve on cooked noodles and garnish with parsley and some freshly grated cheese. A perfect dinner for two.

Angels on Horseback

12 fresh oysters, shucked
6 slices of bacon, cut in half
lemon wedges
12 toothpicks

Preheat oven to 220°C (450°F). Wrap each oyster with a slice of bacon and secure with a toothpick. Bake in preheated oven until the bacon is crispy, eight to ten minutes. Serve immediately.

Select Bibliography

Brooks, William K., *The Oyster* (Baltimore, MD, 1891)

Brown, Helen Evans, *Some Oyster Recipes* (Pasadena, CA, 1951)

Clark, Eleanor, *Oysters of Locmariaquer* (New York, 1956)

De Gouy, Louis P., *The Oyster Book* (New York, 1951)

Fisher, M.F.K., *Consider the Oyster* (New York, 1941)

Greenberg, Paul, *American Catch: The Fight for Our Local Seafood* (New York, 2014)

Guiliano, Mireille, *Meet Paris Oyster: A Love Affair with the Perfect Food* (New York, 2014)

Hedeen, Robert A., *The Oyster: The Life and Lore of the Celebrated Bivalve* (Centreville, MA, 1986)

Jacobsen, Rowan, *A Geography of Oysters: The Connoisseur's Guide to Oyster Eating in North America* (New York, 2007)

Kurlansky, Mark, *The Big Oyster: A Molluscular History of New York* (New York, 2006)

McMurray, Patrick, *Consider the Oyster: A Shucker's Field Guide* (Toronto, 2007)

Philpots, John R., *Oysters, And All About Them, Being a Complete History of the Titular Subject, Exhaustive on All Points of Necessary and Curious Information from the Earliest Writers to those of the Present Time with Numerous Additions, Facts, and Notes* (London, 1890)

Reardon, Joan, *Oysters: A Culinary Celebration* (New York, 2000)

Stott, Rebecca, *Oyster* (London, 2004)

Walsh, Robb, *Sex, Death and Oysters: A Half-shell Lover's World Tour* (Berkeley, CA, 2009)

Williams, Lonnie, and Karen Warner, *Oysters: A Connoisseur's Guide and Cookbook* (Berkeley, CA, 1990)

Websites and Associations

The modern age has provided a new and exciting resource for oyster lovers in the form of mobile phone applications. With GPS technology, a variety of apps now exist to help the oyster lover learn more about oysters and – more importantly – locate oysters in any region they may be attainable. Many oyster bars are developing their own apps to list current offerings. It is worth noting that most of the larger oyster festivals are now developing associated apps to promote the events associated with the festival. These apps often include specific information about dates and timing of the festivals and helpful attendance information such as travel and parking guidance, sponsors, event scheduling and exhibitor information.

Apps

BC Oyster Guide (created by the British Columbia Shellfish Grower's Association)

The BCSGA guide pertains to the British Columbia area of Canada and has sections on 'BC Oyster Directory', 'Identify', 'Where to Find Them', 'Glossary' and 'Photos'. This is a nice app for the 'Where To Find Them' section, not only because it separates out the restaurants by region, but because it includes a link to oyster-centric events.

Oyster Bars

An oyster-bar locator developed by MapMuse that starts by zero-ing in on your location. The user can also filter the search by 'Nearby', 'Location' or 'Name'.

The Oyster Cart

A mobile oyster bar in Singapore moving around and delivering the best oyster party experience for everyone.

Oyster Guru

A somewhat limited guide for identifying East and West Coast oysters from the United States and Canada.

Oysterpedia

Also a U.S.-based app used as a glossary for oyster types. It is affili-ated with The Mermaid Inn in New York City and was established by The Mermaid Inn and Oyster Bar in Manhattan, New York. The Mermaid Inn shucks more than 300,000 oysters each year.

OysterHour

Using GPS technology, this connects users with nearby oyster happy hours.

Oystour

Has listings for Oyster basics, including an Oyster 101 and an Appreciation link. American-centric in its listings.

Websites and Blogs

Food and Agriculture Organization of the United Nations
www.fao.org

In a Half Shell
www.inahalfshell.com

MollusCAN eye
http://molluscan-eye.epoc.u-bordeaux1.fr

Oyster Aficionado
www.oysteraficionado.webs.com

The Oyster Man – Drew Smith
www.theoysterman.blogspot.com

The Oysterman – Brent Petkau
www.theoysterman.com/cms

The Oyster Guide by Rowan Jacobsen
www.oysterguide.com

Oyster Bars and Farms

Oyster Bars

Au Pied d'Cheval – Brittany
10 Quai Gambetta 35260
Cancale, France
+33 2 99 89 76 95

Right on the water and in sight of the oyster farms.

Bentley's
11–15 Swallow Street, Piccadilly
London, UK, W1B 4DG
+44 20 7734 4756

Continuously open since 1914, one of London's oldest oyster bars.

Bentley Oyster Bar and Bistro
20 Dreyer Street, Claremont
Western Cape, South Africa
+27 21 671 3948

Boathouse on Blackwattle Bay

123 Ferry Road, Glebe
New South Wales, 2037, Australia
+61 2 9518 9011

Australia's Sydney Rock is a small oyster with a big, sweet-salty taste. There's no better place to sample it than at the ever-popular Boathouse, set on stilts above a rowing shed on Blackwattle Bay, just an oyster's throw from the Sydney Fish Market (which is another must-visit site, by the way).

Grand Central Oyster Bar

Grand Central Terminal
89 East 42nd Street, New York, New York
+1 212 490 6650
www.oysterbarny.com

Opened in 1913, this is one of America's oldest and grandest oyster bars. With elegant, high-vaulted Guastavino tiled ceilings that seem to shimmer gold and classic, red-checkered tablecloths, this establishment consistently sells more than 2 million oysters a year. Offering upwards of three dozen different varieties, it is a must-visit historical establishment.

Konoba Bako – Croatia

Ulica Ivana Gundulića 1, 21485
Komiža, Croatia
+385 21 713 742

On the pastoral island of Vis, off Croatia's Dalmatian Coast, this harbour-front restaurant has wooden tables inches from the water, with views of the old stone-and-terracotta architecture of Komiža and the rocky, pine-draped mountains beyond.

Moran's The Weir
The Weir, Kilcolgan, County Galway, Ireland
+353 091 796113

Established in 1797 and still owned by the Moran family, 'the weir' was named for an old, nearby wall that was constructed near Dunkellin River to trap salmon. But the locals dredged Galway Bay oysters and their thirst was only sated by a pint of Guinness. It remains one of the most iconic oyster bars in all of Ireland.

Rodney's Oyster House
469 King Street West
Toronto, ON M5V 1K4, Canada
+1 416 363 8105

Sydney Cove Oyster Bar
Lot 1, Circular Quay East
Sydney, Australia
+61 02 9247 2937

Swan Oyster Depot
1517 Polk Street, San Francisco, California
+1 415 673 1101

Only open for lunch, there is always a line out the door of this small, historic oyster bar that has been in continuous operation since 1912. There are only twelve seats and the queue for those precious spots at the marble counter starts building half an hour before they open. Originally opened by four Danish brothers, Sal Sancimino and his cousins purchased the business in 1946 and it is Sal's six sons who are still running the business to this day.

Oyster Farms and Museums Open to the Public

Both Hog Island Oyster Farm and Tomales Bay Oyster Company operate in Marshall, California

Hog Island
20215 Shoreline Highway, Marshall, California
+1 415 663 9218
http://hogislandoysters.com/visit/marshall

Island Creek
Aboard an oyster skiff, their tour includes upwellers, the nursery, the back river, harvesting and processing. And the Oysterplex.

Duxbury, Massachusetts, 02331
781-934-2028
http://islandcreekoysters.com/ico/farm/farm-visit

Le Musée de l'Etang de Thau
Pier fishing port 34140
Bouzigues, France
+33 4 67 78 33 57
www.bouzigues.fr/musee

Taylor Shellfish Farms
130 South East Lynch Road, Shelton, Washington, 98584
+1 360 426 6178
www.taylorshellfishfarms.com

Tomales Bay
15479 Highway One, Marshall, United States
+1 415 663 1243
www.tomalesbayoystercompany.com

Oyster Festivals

Month	Country	State/County	Festival Name
January	U.S.	South Carolina	Charleston Lowcountry Oyster Festival
February	U.S.	Vermont	Bluebird Tavern Oyster Festival
	Japan	Hiroshima	Miyajima Oyster Festival
March	Croatia	Dubrovnik	Fešta od Kamenica
April	U.S.	Texas	San Antonio Fiesta Oyster Bake
May	Australia	New South Wales	Narooma Oyster Festival
	New Zealand	Bluff	Bluff Oyster Festival
June	U.S.	Louisiana	New Orleans Oyster Festival
	England	Colchester	Oyster Fayre
	Canada	Comox	Comox Valley Shellfish Festival
July	England	Whitstable	Whitstable Oyster Festival
	France	Riec-sur-Belon	La fête de l'huître

July	South Africa	Knysna	Knysna Oyster Festival
August	Canada	Prince Edward Island	Tyne Valley Oyster Festival
	U.S.	Connecticut	Milford Oyster Festival
	Ireland	Ballylongford	Ballylongford Oyster Festival
September	U.S.	New York	New York Oyster Week
	U.S.	Illinois	Guinness Chicago Oyster Fest
	Australia	Ceduna	Ceduna Oysterfest
	Ireland	Galway	Galway International Oyster Festival
	Northern Ireland	Hillsborough	Hillsborough Oyster Festival
	England	Woburn	Woburn Oyster Festival
October	U.S.	Maryland	St Mary's County Oyster Festival
	U.S.	California	Morro Bay/Central Coast Oyster Festival
	U.S.	Massachusetts	Wellfleet OysterFest
	England	Falmouth	Falmouth Oyster Festival
	Brazil	Florianópolis	Fenaostra
November	U.S.	Florida	Apalachicola Florida Seafood Festival

Month	Country	Location	Festival
November	U.S.	Virginia	Urbanna Oyster Festival
	Australia	Brisbane	Brisbane Water Oyster Festival
December	U.S.	South Carolina	Johns Island Oyster Fest

Acknowledgements

I am truly beholden to so many people in assisting with this endeavour. For giving me invaluable, first-hand experience with their oysters, I am grateful to Gabe Trujillo of ABS Seafood, Lory Stewart and Francis Santos of Detail Fish Aquaculture in Provincetown, Massachusetts, Andrew Cummings of the Massachusetts Aquaculture Association and Dennis Peterson of Carlsbad Aquafarm in Carlsbad, California. For being my go-to guru and answering innumerable questions, Brent Petkau, The Oyster Man, I raise a glass and toast you, my friend.

Thanks to Tammy Reynard and Scott of The Fossil Forum for their guidance in all things ancient and mysterious. For culinary historical information and guidance: Ken Albala of the University of the Pacific, Andrew Coe, Andrew Smith and all the culinary historians on Facebook who answered questions in the middle of the night. Special thanks to Celia Sack of Omnivore Books for allowing me into her amazing personal library.

For being my first cheerleader and all around great Surrogate Mom, thank you Paula Wolfert, and her husband, Art Buddy, Bill Bayer!

I can't thank enough all my close friends who assisted, cajoled, shopped, ate, inspired and stood by me during the process: Maria Lorraine Binchet, Philip Carli, Joan Chyun, Rob and Leisl Cluff, Jerry Kajpust, BFF (Best-Foodie-Friend) Lisa Lowitz, Dio Luria, Ralph Maldonado, Laura Martin-Bacon, Ellen Matheson, Tom Riedel, Heather Vail and Lance Wright.

Very, very special thanks to Richard Foss for encouragement, research and guidance. To Martha Jay for her infinite patience and counsel. And to my sister, Susan Wood – for all you do.

I give thumbs-up to my new family, Becca and Daniel, for their willingness to taste any dish I cooked for them and lastly – but most earnestly – to my beloved husband, Andrew Calman, for being the priceless pearl in my oyster of life.

Photo Acknowledgements

The author and publishers wish to express their thanks to the below sources of illustrative material and/or permission to reproduce it. Some locations of artworks are also given below, in the interests of brevity.

Photo Ammodramus (made available under the Creative Commons CC0 1.0 Universal Public Domain Dedication): p. 64; photo Jan Arkesteijn: p. 69; photo BeatrixBelibaste: p. 59; courtesy Joost Bos/ The Prints Collector: p. 53; courtesy Campbell's Soup Company: p. 105; licensed by the Chesapeake Bay Program, Annapolis, Maryland, and reproduced by kind permission: p. 21 (top); The Chincoteague Museum, Virginia: p. 99; courtesy Rob Cluff: p. 128; reproduced courtesy The Corning Museum of Glass, New York: p. 35; photos Dcoetzee: pp. 56, 57, 80; courtesy Diageo PLC: p. 108; photo Steve Droter: p. 21 (top); photos Lewis Wickes Hine (Library of Congress, Washington, DC – Prints and Photographs Division, from the records of the National Child Labor Committee): pp. 74, 75; photo Robert Kerton: p. 20; photo Maksym Kravtsov: p. 134; photo Los Angeles Country Museum of Art: p. 61; courtesy Patrick McMurphy (aka Paddy Shucker): p. 8; Mauritshuis, Den Haag: p. 117; Photo Maxshimasu: p. 114; from Eustace Clare Grenville Murray, *The Oyster; Where, How and When to Find, Breed, Cook, and Eat It* (London, 1861): pp. 50, 86: Musée Condé, Chantilly: p. 57; Musée d'Orsay, Paris: p. 114; Museo del Prado, Madrid: p. 59; Muzeum Narodowe, Wrocław, Poland: p. 69; photo Nationaal

Index

italic numbers refer to illustrations; **bold** to recipes